Handcrafted designs & techniques

WIREWORK
JEWELRY WORKSHOP

Sian Hamilton

First published 2015 by
Guild of Master Craftsman Publications Ltd
Castle Place, 166 High Street, Lewes,
East Sussex BN7 1XU

Text © GMC Publications, 2015
Copyright in the Work © GMC Publications Ltd, 2015

Step photography by the jewelry designers; all other
photography by Laurel Guilfoyle.

ISBN 978 1 86108 763 8

Publisher Jonathan Bailey
Production Manager Jim Bulley
Senior Project Editor Dominique Page
Editor Ruth O'Rourke-Jones
Managing Art Editor Gilda Pacitti
Designer Ginny Zeal

Set in ITC Century BT

Color origination by GMC Reprographics

Printed and bound by in China

Contents

INTRODUCTION

Jewelry making is a fun and easy hobby to learn. It can be as complicated or simple as you want it to be. In recent years, wirework has become one of the most popular jewelry disciplines to master, and it really can be super simple or quite technically challenging. If you stick at it, you can create pieces with a real wow factor. Start with the easier projects and leave the complicated wire weaving until you have a few practice projects under your belt. Remember, at the beginning of your journey with wirework, plated metal wires are your friend and far more cost-effective when practicing.

I am Sian Hamilton and I have been making jewelry for over 30 years. From the string of plastic beads I made as a child and wore with pride, through to a BA (honours) degree in 3D design specializing in jewelry I have been immersed in design my entire life. These days I make and sell jewelry by commission, have recently written a couple of books about jewelry making, and am also the editor of *Making Jewellery,* a magazine for jewelry makers. Many amazingly talented designers create beautiful projects for the magazine. It is these designers who have created the awesome projects in this book.

Wire is a simple product and can be found throughout the home in many forms. So, if you are re-decorating, remember to check out old appliances for bits of wire or strip old electrical wire to use in projects. Copper is one of the greatest metals for making lovely warm-toned pieces. As you move onward and upward in your skill level, consider sterling silver wire as an option. Due to the higher price, it's a metal that is best used when you are more confident in your ability, as you don't want to waste it. The advantage of sterling silver wire over plated wire is that it will last almost forever!

Tools & Equipment

Here is a selection of the most commonly used tools and equipment you will need to make all the projects in this book.

PLIERS AND CUTTERS

1 Round-nose pliers
These pliers have round jaws that taper to the end and are used for making jumprings, eyepins, loops, and spirals.

2 Chain-nose pliers
Sometimes known as snipe-nose, these pliers have flat jaws that taper at the end. They are useful for holding small pieces of wire.

3 Flat-nose pliers
These pliers have flat jaws that do not taper. They are used for holding wire flat while working and opening and closing jumprings.

4 Nylon-nose pliers
These have nylon-coated jaws that don't make marks in the wire when holding pieces tight.

5 Looping pliers
These have one round jaw (sometimes stepped), opposite a curved jaw that the round one sits into. They are used for making wrapped and simple loops with ease.

6 Bail-making pliers
These have two round jaws that are an even width all the way along the plier jaws (unlike round-nose pliers that taper). They come in a range of sizes measured in millimetres and each jaw is a different size—usually 1–2mm apart.

7 Side cutters
These cutters have the cutting jaw on the side. Flush cutters give a fairly straight cut and are an essential wirework tool.

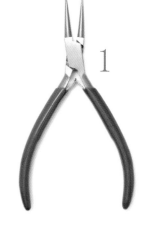

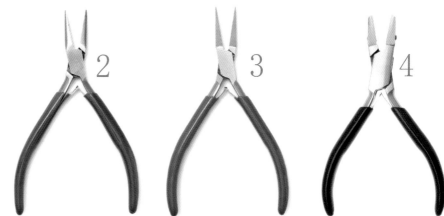

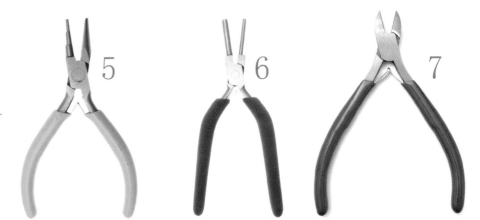

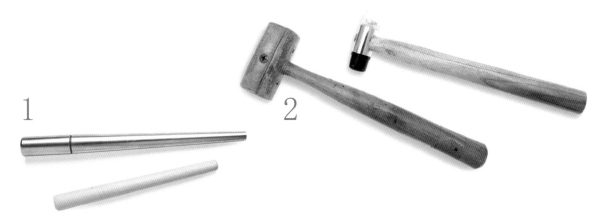

MANDRELS

1 Mandrels

These are used for forming jewelry items into a particular shape. Mandrels can be made of wood, metal or plastic. They come in many shapes and sizes for rings, bracelets and bezels. They are often tapered or stepped (often known as multi-mandrels). Ring mandrels may have sizes marked on the side.

HAMMERS AND MALLETS

There are many types of jewelry hammer. In general, all you need is one with a rounded end and one with a flat end so you can add texture or flatten wire.

2 Mallets

Mallets come with different heads—those most commonly used in jewelry making are rawhide and nylon. Either is good for hardening wire with a steel block.

THE REST

3 Steel block

This is a flat piece of steel used to hit wire on with a hammer or mallet to flatten or harden it.

4 Wooden ring vice

A vice will hold your wire in place and make it easier to handle. Made of wood, it has a hinge in the middle and a wooden wedge that you push in the opposite side to hold the jewelry.

5 Files and emery paper

It's good to have a couple of fine files for rounding sharp ends of wires, and emery (or sand) paper to smooth the wire off.

6 Liver of sulfur

This is a chemical that darkens metals including silver and copper. It is mixed with water, then the piece is dipped in the solution and becomes darker the longer it stays in. The patina can be removed by using a metal-polishing cloth. Liver of sulfur does not work on some metals, including gold or brass.

7 Adhesive

Fix wire ends so they don't catch on skin with a liquid adhesive formulated for jewelry use such as GS Hypo cement. Avoid cyanoacrylate adhesive (also known as superglue) as it can react with metals. Industrial thick adhesive such as E6000 is used where pieces need to be stuck together permanently. Take care to use adhesives in a well-ventilated area.

Materials

The projects in this book are made using materials that are easy to track down and reasonably cheap to buy.

STRINGING MATERIALS

1 Wire
The main material in wirework projects is wire, and it comes in a huge variety of sizes, shapes, and colors. Wire is measured differently in the UK, Europe, and the USA. Below is a chart of the main sizes. AWG is American Wire Gauge (called US gauge in this book), MM is the millimeter size, and SWG is Standard Wire Gauge, which is sometimes used in Europe. In the step instructions throughout this book, we will refer to the US gauge size, but please see the materials list at the start of each project for all conversions.

AWG	MM	SWG
10	2.5mm	12
12	2mm	14
14	1.5mm	16
16	1.25mm	18
18	1mm	19
20	0.8mm	21
22	0.6mm	23
24	0.5mm	25
26	0.4mm	27
28	0.3mm	30

2 Nylon-coated wire
This wire is particularly good for stringing, as it has a better strength for heavy beads than ordinary threads.

3 Leather/cord/suede
These types of cords come in various colors and thicknesses. They can be knotted securely with ease or used with ribbon crimps or neck ends.

4 Chain
There are many styles of chain, from very fine to large and chunky, and they come in a variety of colors. Pick a chain to suit the weight of the items you are hanging from it.

5 Memory wire
Memory wire comes in necklace and bracelet sizes. It is a very hard wire that has been created to hold its shape. You can pull it apart to thread on beads and when you let go of the wire, it will reform into a circle.

EMBELLISHMENTS

1 Beads
There is such a large variety of beads available, from tiny seed beads to large handmade, lampwork glass ones. Beads can be made from plastic (also called Lucite), pearl, wood, metal, glass, resin, or crystal.

2 Crystals
Crystals come as beads, pendants, buttons, flat-back stones, and pointed-back stones (called chatons). They are beautiful and add sparkle to designs.

FINDINGS

Findings are all the items you use to make up jewelry other than beads, pendants, or charms.

3 Jumprings
A jumpring is a single ring of wire that is used to join pieces together. They come in every size you can think of and in many colors.

4 Headpins
These are pieces of wire with a flat or ball end (headpin) or a loop at the end (eyepin). Headpins are used with beads to hang them on jewelry and eyepins to make a chain.

5 Earwires
Earwires come in various styles, from a simple "U"-shape with a loop, to ones with a bead and coil finish.

6 Clasps
A TRIGGER
Also known as a lobster or parrot clasp, these are the most widely used clasps on the market.

B BOLT RING
Similar to the trigger clasp, the spring-closing mechanism pushes a bar across the opening.

C MAGNETIC
These are great for bracelets when making them for yourself or for any person who finds opening and closing clasps difficult. Magnets will attach to some base metals, such as plated chains.

D PUSH BUTTON
These clasps have a ball on one side and a ring on the other. Both sides have loops to attach to necklaces. The ball pushes through the ring and holds the piece closed.

E TOGGLE
A great choice when making the clasp a feature of your design, these have a loop on one end and a bar that fits through the loop to attach to the other end.

7 Sieves
These are shallow domes of metal with holes that you can attach decorations to. Sieves come as rings, brooches, or plain to attach to jumprings. They often come with a backing plate with small hinges to attach the sieve.

8 Brooch back or bar
This is a brooch pin on a bar that has holes to attach it to the piece being made as a brooch. It can be sewn on, attached with wire, or glued.

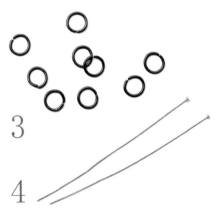

Techniques

The following pages will illustrate some of the basic techniques needed to make your own jewelry and complete the projects in this book.

Opening and closing a jumpring

To make sure that jumprings shut securely, it is important to know how to open and close them correctly. You will need two pairs of pliers with flat jaws—chain-nose or flat-nose pliers will work.

1 Take a jumpring with the opening centered at the top and hold in two pairs of pliers. Holding the jumpring this way—with one pair of pliers across one side of the ring—helps to stabilize large rings.

2 You can also hold the pliers this way, with both pairs facing inward. Both ways are fine, and the way you need to attach the jumpring often dictates how you hold it.

3 Hold the jumpring on both sides and twist one hand toward you and the other hand away. This will keep the ring round in shape. Reverse the action to close the ring. Don't ever pull the ring apart as that will warp the shape. Use this technique to open loops on eyepins too.

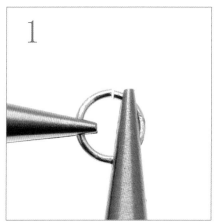

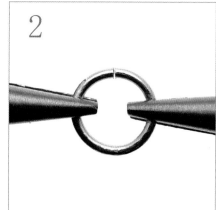

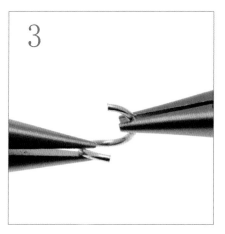

If you find your pliers mark the jumprings, wrap a bit of masking tape around the ends.

Making a simple loop

Loops have a multitude of functions in making jewelry so forming them properly is a skill worth mastering. A simple (sometimes called open) loop can be opened and closed to allow it to be attached and detached as desired.

1 Thread the bead onto a head- or eyepin and cut the pin about ⅜in (10mm) above the bead.

2 Bend the wire to a right angle above the bead.

3 Using round-nose pliers, grasp the wire at the very end and curl it around the plier jaws.

4 Roll the wire around to meet the bead.

5 Move the plier jaws around the loop to sit by the bead, away from the open end. Bend the loop back to sit directly above the bead.

6 Use chain-nose pliers to tighten the loop by wiggling it until the gap is closed.

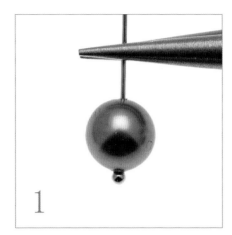

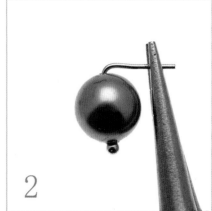

Making a wrapped loop

1

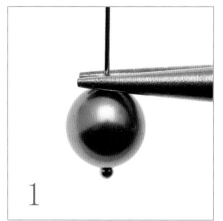

2

3

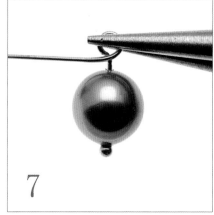

6

7

8

This style of loop is the most secure. Once attached, it cannot be removed unless it is cut off.

1 Thread a bead onto a head- or eyepin. Grip the wire with round-nose pliers next to the bead.

2 Bend the wire above the plier jaw to a right angle. You will need about ⅛in (2mm) of wire above the bead before the bend.

3 Move the plier jaws to sit at the top of the bend.

4 With your thumb, push the wire back around the pliers, keeping it tight to the jaw.

5 Keep pushing the wire around the jaw until you meet the bead.

6 Move the pliers around the loop to hold it close to the open side. Continue to bend the wire around until it is facing out at a right angle and you have a complete loop.

7 Use a pair of chain-nose pliers to hold across the loop firmly. Make sure any chain or ring is above the pliers. If adding the loop to chain or a jumpring, thread the loop onto the chain at this stage

8 Wrap the wire around the neck of the loop until it meets the bead.

9 Take side cutters and snip off any excess wire. Make sure the flat side of the cutter jaws is facing the coil.

10 Take the chain-nose pliers and push the cut end of the wire into the coil, so it sits flush.

Making a spiral

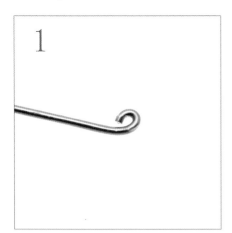

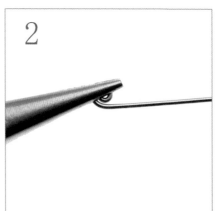

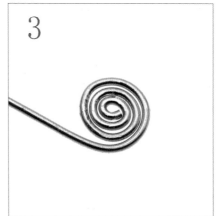

A spiral is a good alternative to a simple headpin to decorate pieces.

1 Take a length of wire. With round-nose pliers, bend the very tip around in a loop.

2 Place the loop flat in the jaws of chain-nose pliers and push the wire against the loop.

3 Work round in a circle, moving the loop in the chain-nose pliers. Allow the wire to coil around the outside of the loop to make your spiral.

BASIC WIREWORK WEAVES

Once you know how to achieve the basic weaves, you can do so much with wirework. The following steps show three basic weaves, for two-wire, three-wire and four-frames. To keep the weaving tidy, use US 28-gauge (SWG 30, 0.3mm) wire for the weaving and US 18-gauge (SWG 19, 1mm) wire for the frames.

Two-wire

Three-wire

Four-wire

Two-wire

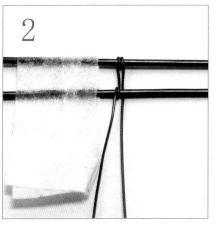

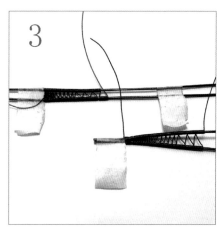

1 To prepare the wires, lay them parallel at the required distance apart and use small pieces of low-tack masking tape to maintain the gap. This weave works with parallel frame wires, any distance apart that you need. Frames for a graduated shape can be prepared by taping one end together. The weave also works with curved wires, by weaving an extra coil around the larger curved frame wire.

2 Coil the weaving wire once around the lower frame wire, coiling away from you. Pass the wire in front of the lower wire and behind the upper wire and coil twice around the upper wire, toward you. Pass the wire in front of the upper wire, behind the lower wire and coil twice, away from you. Continue like this until you have the required length of woven wire.

3 The first section of weaving in the picture above is made with two coils between each pass. The center section is achieved by coiling five times between passes. The widest section uses ten coils between each pass of the weave. The look of this weave can easily be varied by increasing the number of coils between each pass.

Three-wire

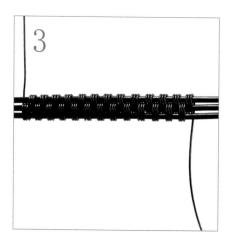

1 Begin with two of the three straight-frame wires parallel and adjacent to each other. Use your weaving wire to coil around both of these wires together three times. Then bring the weaving wire between the two frame wires, ready to continue the weave.

2 Lay the third straight-frame wire above the two previously coiled wires. Coil the weaving wire around this wire, and the center wire together, three times. After the third coil, take the weaving wire behind all three of your frame wires and continue to weave, alternating coiling three times around the lower and the center wires together and the center and the upper wires together.

3 Continue weaving in this way until you have the length required for your project. This weave bends and holds a shape well, so is particularly good for making shapes. It works equally well with curves and circular shapes and angular shapes. It may be easier to weave with the wires straight, then form the woven wires into the required shape, rather than to weave shaped wires.

Four-wire

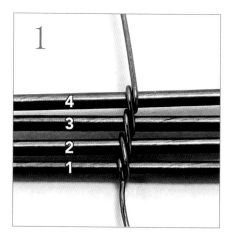

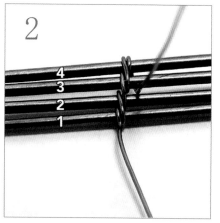

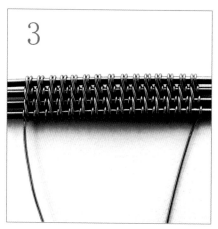

1 Line the frame wires up parallel and weave away from yourself as follows: Coil once around wire 1, then pass the wire across wire 2 and coil once around it. Pass across wire 3 and coil once around it, pass across wire 4 and coil once around it, then coil once more around wire 4.

2 As you come back down the wires, weave toward yourself, around wire 4, then—passing behind each wire before you coil—around wires 3, 2, and 1 respectively, finishing with one more coil around wire 1. You can use as many frame wires with this weave as you need to achieve the width required for your project. Four have been used here as an example.

3 Continue weaving until you have the length required for your project. This is a sturdy weave, and is great for making bracelets and cuffs because the close weave holds the frame wires rigid. It is also particularly effective with colored wire on a plain base, such as copper or gunmetal, as this shows the pattern of the weave up well. The weave works best for straight designs.

Hardening wire

Lots of the projects in this book ask you to harden the wire so that it doesn't bend (and possibly snap) when the jewelry piece is being worn. It's really easy to do following these steps.

1 Take either a rawhide or nylon-head mallet and a steel block. Lay the wire to be hardened on the steel block and firmly hit it with the hammer.

2 Hammer straight down on the wire to get as much impact as possible, making sure the wire is flat against the steel block.

Flush cutting

Getting flat ends on wire is easy if you use the cutters in the right way.

1 All cutters have a flat side, as seen here…

2 …and an angled side, as seen here.

3 To cut wire with a flat end you need to work with the flat side of the pliers.

4 Hold the wire at a right angle to the cutters with the end you are going to be using on your jewelry piece facing the flat side of the pliers.

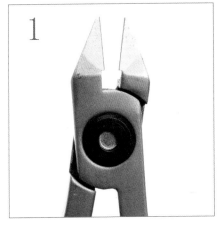

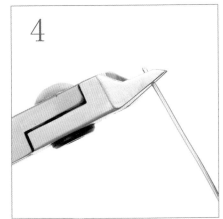

Using liver of sulfur

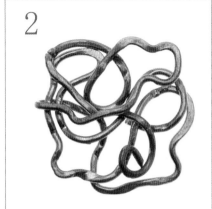

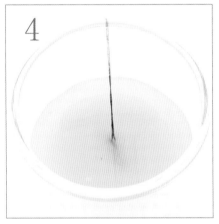

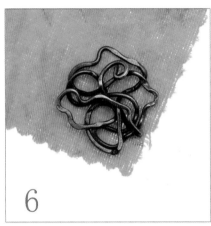

Liver of sulfur (LOS) is a substance used to produce a patina that darkens metals. It works on silver, copper, and bronze.

1   To use LOS you will need two water containers (in the step photos small glasses have been used, but you can use anything that can take water and that you don't use with food), a pair of plastic tweezers, some paper tissue, and bicarbonate of soda. It is important to follow the safety instructions that come with LOS, so you will also need safety glasses and gloves. Always work in a well-ventilated area, as although LOS is non-toxic it smells very bad! Clean the item to be colored in hot soapy water to wash off any grease or residue from the making process.

2   For this demonstration a length of bare copper wire has been used, crunched up to add a few layers and give the piece interest.

3   Half-fill one water container with cold water and the other with warm, not boiling, water from the faucet. LOS can also be used with cold water, but it takes far longer for the color to develop. You only need a few drops of LOS for this process—the stronger the solution the blacker the results.

4   Dip the piece on the thread into the LOS, making sure the whole piece is just covered or the patina will not develop evenly. Hold it in the solution until it turns the color you want it to go. If you are not sure, periodically take it out and dunk it in the cold water to stop the coloring process and take a look at the piece. You can keep going back to the LOS solution as many times as you like.

5   When the piece is the required color, mix some fresh water with a little baking soda and dip the piece in to neutralize the LOS. Then wash the piece thoroughly using liquid dish soap and warm water.

6   Allow the piece to air dry, then use a polishing cloth to take the patina off the top surface. LOS is a great way to make patterns show up, and polishing off the dark color from the surface of the piece adds to the effect. Over time, the patina may darken or become lighter. To prevent this, coat the piece with a layer of wax or an appropriate varnish.

Spring Burst

Put a spring in your step with this pretty pendant and ring set by Laura Binding, which combines wire with clusters of beads, flowers, leaves, and butterflies.

FOR THE PENDANT YOU WILL NEED

1 x reel of US 18-gauge (SWG 19, 1mm) wire, silver-plated

1 x 39⅜in (1m) length of US 26-gauge (SWG 27, 0.4mm) wire, silver-plated

3 x Lucite leaf beads

10 x small, Lucite bell-shape flowers

7 x small butterfly beads

5 x 4mm beads

3 x 6mm jumprings

6 x 4mm jumprings

22 x 1in (25mm) headpins, silver-colored

1 x 6in (150mm) medium curb chain

1 x ready-made chain

Side cutters

Round-nose pliers

Chain-nose pliers

Bail-making pliers or ring mandrel

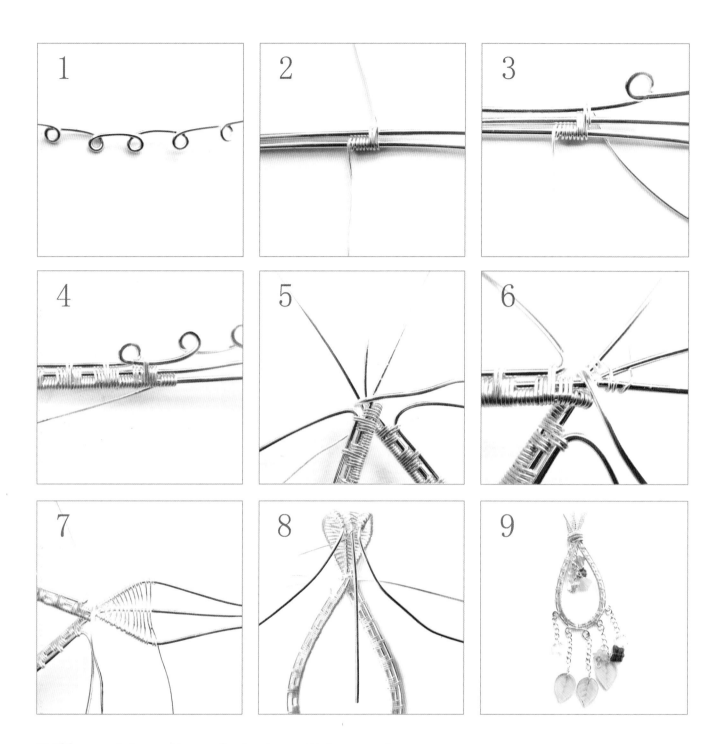

Different lengths of chain will impact
on the look of this piece. A longer chain
will make a statement when worn over
a high-neck dress or top.

Pendant

1   Cut 14in (355mm) of 18-gauge wire and bring the ends together to form a "U" shape. Place the round-nose pliers in the middle and bring the two ends around to form a loop. This will be your center loop. Straighten the wire with your fingers and measure ⅜in (10mm) and repeat with another loop on one side of the center loop. Make two loops on both sides of the center loops.

2   Cut 12in (305mm) of 18-gauge wire and add a bend at the end. Use 26-gauge wire (keeping it on the reel will reduce having to cut and add) and anchor it onto the end of the wire. Leave a small tail and wrap the wire five times. Cut another 12in (305mm) of 18-gauge wire and place that above the first piece and wrap the 26-gauge wire over both the wires three times.

3   Add the first wire you made the loops on and place on top of the two wires. Bring the 26-gauge wire up over all three wires and wrap twice. Bring the wire back down, then wrap it around just the middle and bottom wire three times. Take it back to the first wire and wrap this five times. You will have created a spike effect.

4   Check that the tension stays even as you weave so that all three thick wires sit in a row. If the thick wires pull together, use pliers to pull them apart. After you have created seven spikes, move the weave to sit next to the first loop on the top wire. Continue the pattern, weaving in between the loops. Repeat with another seven spikes after the loops.

5   Still with the 26-gauge wire on the reel, gently form the completed frame into an oval, crossing the ends of the wire one in front of the other. Bend the wires on the outside edge (the one with the loops) on both sides and bring them down. Take another outer wire and wrap it around the three central wires. Position these wires in a fan shape to create the bail.

6   Bring the 26-gauge wire up to the outer bail wire and wrap it around the wire once, then wrap it around again before bringing it into the middle to go to the other bail wire. Because you have a third wire in the middle, simply go over the wire to the other side and wrap it around once, then around again back to the other side going under the middle wire.

7   To form the bail, continue weaving until you have the height of your bail, then use the chain-nose pliers and push the weave as close as you can. Bend the two outer wires in toward each other. Tease out the ends to create a diamond shape and continue weaving up the other side to create the rest of the bail.

8   Ease the two outer wires apart slightly using bail-making pliers or a ring mandrel. At the diamond point of the bail, gently form it over, so the wires are at the back. Bring the outer wires to the front, then wrap them both around the whole bail again. When they are at the front, trim them.

9   Cut the middle wire from the bail about ⅜in (10mm) and form into a small loop, add some chain, and close the loop. Trim the excess wires leaving one side wire. With the 26-gauge wire, hand coil the side wires, and use this to wrap around the bail and cover the ends you cut from the bail. Add chain to the loops and beads to the chain.

Ring

YOU WILL NEED

1 x 20in (510mm) length of US 20-gauge (SWG 21, 0.8mm) wire, silver-colored

20 x 4mm round beads

20 x 1in (25mm) headpins, silver-colored

Take a 12in (305mm) piece of 20-gauge wire and, using round-nose pliers, create three loops roughly in the middle of the wire. Wrap the wire three times around a mandrel using the loops as the top. Take the ring off the mandrel and coil the ends of the wire around the ring by the outside of the three loops, cut off any excess, and press the ends in with chain-nose pliers. Add beads to headpins and make simple loops on the ends of the pins (see page 15). Attach the loops to the three loops on the ring and twist the headpin loops to open them. Thread onto one of the three loops to form a charm ring. Place as many headpin loops on each ring loop as you can, to make a nice cluster.

Celtic Knot

The twists and turns of this wire knot evoke simpler times.
Sue Mason-Burns has teamed her take on the Celtic knot
with some natural wooden beads to create a striking collection.

FOR THE NECKLACE YOU WILL NEED

1 x reel of US 16-gauge (SWG 18,1.25mm) wire, copper

1 x reel of US 26-gauge (SWG 27, 0.4mm) wire, copper

6 x 20mm x 4mm jackfruit (nangka) wood slide-cut beads

6 x 1in (25mm) copper eyepins

11 x 5mm jumprings, copper

1 x 8mm jumpring, copper

1 x reel of chain, antique copper

1 x trigger clasp, copper

Liver of sulfur

Side cutters

Small bail-making pliers

Round-nose pliers

Chain-nose pliers

Hammer

Steel bench block

Earrings

YOU WILL NEED

8 x 1½in (40mm) lengths of US 18-gauge (SWG 19, 1mm) wire, copper

2 x 10in (250mm) lengths of US 26-gauge (SWG 27, 0.4mm) wire, copper

2 x earwires, copper

Make two of the Celtic knot designs using smaller dimensions and hang from handmade earwires.

Necklace

1 Flush cut four 2½in (60mm) lengths of 16-gauge wire. Using the larger jaw of small bail-making pliers, turn an inward loop to each end of the four bent wires by grasping the end of the wire in the jaw of the pliers and wrapping the wire around the larger jaw to make a "P" shape. Hammer each of the four wire shapes flat using a hammer on a steel bench block. Use the bail-making pliers to close the loops, which may have opened slightly during hammering.

2 Lay out the design of the Celtic knot by placing two of the shapes together, with the flat sides running parallel and the loops turning away from each other. Place the remaining two shapes in the same way, laying them across your first two shapes so that they form the circular shape.

3 To lash the two sets of two wires together, cut a 20in (500mm) length of 26-gauge copper wire. Leave a small tail and wrap it three times diagonally across both sets of the two flattened wires. Turn the design once to the right and wrap three times on the opposite diagonal. Wrap each set of two flat wires together three times. Finish by threading the tail wire through the wrapping wires at the back and trimming both tails.

4 Prepare a mixture of lukewarm water and a couple of drops of liver of sulfur in a non-metallic bowl. Prepare a separate bowl of cold water. Tie a small piece of string around each of the copper shapes. Dip each in turn into the liver of sulfur solution first, then the cold water. Repeat this process until you have achieved the level of oxidation you require. See page 21 for extra information.

5 Take an eyepin, thread on a wooden slide-cut bead and finish with a simple loop in the opposite side (see page 15). Make six of these connector beads. Assemble the necklace, alternating knot shapes and connector beads, attaching the loops of the connector beads to the loops of the knot shapes with jumprings (see page 14).

6 Make the necklace up to the desired length by attaching equal-length pieces of antique copper chain to the loop of the last connector bead on each side. Finish one end of the chain by attaching a trigger clasp with a 5mm jumpring. Attach an 8mm jumpring to connect the clasp and the remaining length of chain.

Be sure to use bare copper wire, as tarnish-free wire will not oxidize in the liver of sulfur solution.

1

2

3

4

5

6

Bracelet

YOU WILL NEED

8 x 1½in (38mm) US 18-gauge (SWG 19, 1mm) wire, copper

2 x 10in (250mm) lengths of US 26-gauge (SWG 27, 0.4mm) wire, copper

15 x 4mm jumprings, copper

4 x 2in (50mm) eyepins, copper

4 x 20mm x 4mm jackfruit (nangka) wood slide-cut beads

1 x toggle clasp, antique copper

Use the same techniques as you used for the necklace to make a matching bracelet. Attach the connector beads through two loops of the knot shapes using two jumprings rather than one. Finish with a matching toggle clasp.

When hammering, use the flat side if you want your shape to be perfectly flat, and the rounded side to add texture to your design.

Wrapped Up

Make beautiful wire-wrapped shapes clustered with topaz, citrine, and aquamarine gemstones for this sparkling, pretty set by Jessica Rose.

FOR THE NECKLACE
YOU WILL NEED

1 x 12in (300mm) length of US 16-gauge (SWG 18, 1.25mm) wire, gold-plated

1 x 33–66ft (10–20m) length of US 26-gauge (SWG 27, 0.4mm) wire, gold-plated

1 x 40in (1m) length of thin chain, gold-plated

Mixture of beads and briolettes (topaz, citrine, aquamarine, labradorite, clear crystal, and gold-plated)

Round-nose pliers

Chain-nose pliers

Side cutters

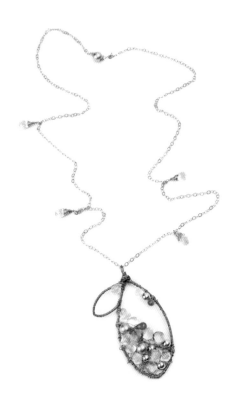

Earrings

YOU WILL NEED

1 x 12in (305mm) length of US 16-gauge (SWG 18, 1.25mm) wire, gold-colored

1 x 16in (405mm) length of US 26-gauge (SWG 27, 0.4mm) wire, gold-colored

2 x 10mm briolettes, blue topaz

2 x earwires, gold-colored

Make a simple pair of matching earrings by creating two drop-shaped frames from 16-gauge gold-plated wire. Wrap the 26-gauge wire around the whole frame, as in the necklace, and add a topaz briolette to each one. Finally, add a pair of earwires.

Necklace

1. Using the side cutters, cut off around 10in (250mm) of 16-gauge wire for the framework. With round-nose pliers, bend the wire near the middle to create a leaf-like shape using the natural curve of the wire.

2. Where the wires cross at the top, wrap one around the other, using chain-nose pliers to secure the shape. After a few wraps, cut off the wire as close to the wraps as possible, then squash the end in using chain-nose pliers. Wrap the remaining stalk of wire over the round-nose pliers to make a loop to hang the pendant on.

3. Using a new piece of 16-gauge wire about 6in (150mm) long, repeat to make a smaller leaf shape. Wrap the wires at the top to secure. Attach the smaller leaf to the larger one using the remaining stalk of wire by wrapping it around the wraps below the bail loop. Cut off any wire ends and squash the ends in with pliers.

4. Cut off a long piece of 26-gauge wire and begin wrapping it around the whole frame of the piece. This will also help to secure the smaller leaf shape to the larger one. Keep your wires tidy as you work and wrap them tightly next to each other. Squash in any wire ends with pliers.

5. Wrap a new piece of 26-gauge wire around the base a few times to secure it, then add the beads and briolettes, one by one. Make sure you are happy with the position of each bead before adding the next.

6. Put in place a few guide wires across the large leaf shape to support the beads as you add them. Still using 26-gauge wire, wrap it around the frame in a zigzag shape and continue to fill in the shape with your beads until you are happy with the design.

7. Using a new piece of 26-gauge wire, add a blue topaz briolette to the small leaf shape for decoration. In the example, three more beads have been added to the top right side of the piece, but you can be creative and use the wire to wrap beads wherever you like within the frame of the leaves.

8. Thread 40in (1m) of thin gold-plated chain through the loop at the top of the piece using 26-gauge wire. For additional sparkle, add briolettes to the chain by threading each onto a 5in (124mm) length of 26-gauge wire and making a small loop above the bead. Thread loop through a link in the chain and wrap wire back around the loop and down over the top of the briolette. Cut off any excess.

9. Cut the end of the chain to the desired length and join the two ends together with a bead and looped wire at each end (see page 15). This is a long necklace that can be put over the head. If you are making a shorter necklace, add a clasp at this point.

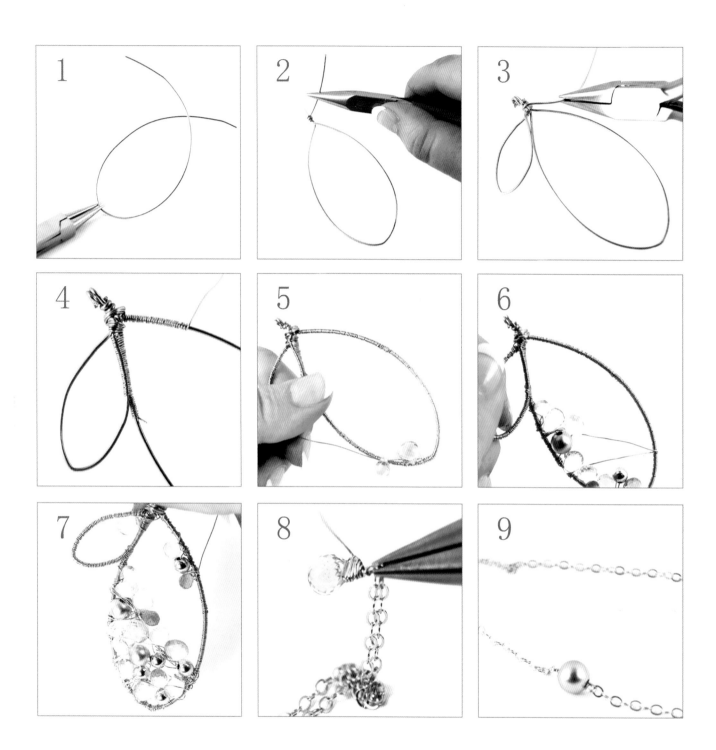

Wire Heart

Wear your heart on your sleeve with this pretty brooch by Sue Mason-Burns, and team it with the gorgeous matching earrings. Let your imagination run wild with sumptuous shades of purple crystals and decorative copper.

FOR THE BROOCH
YOU WILL NEED

1 x reel of US 18-gauge (SWG 19, 1mm) wire, copper

1 x reel of US 28-gauge (SWG 30, 0.3mm) wire, copper

1 x large metal flower bead

1 x small metal flower bead

5 x 8mm faceted glass beads, purple

6 x 6mm beads, amethyst

14 x 4mm bicone crystals, purple

10 x 3mm faceted Czech fire-polished beads, purple

1 x 1¾₁₆in (30mm) brooch pin

Round-nose pliers

Ring mandrel

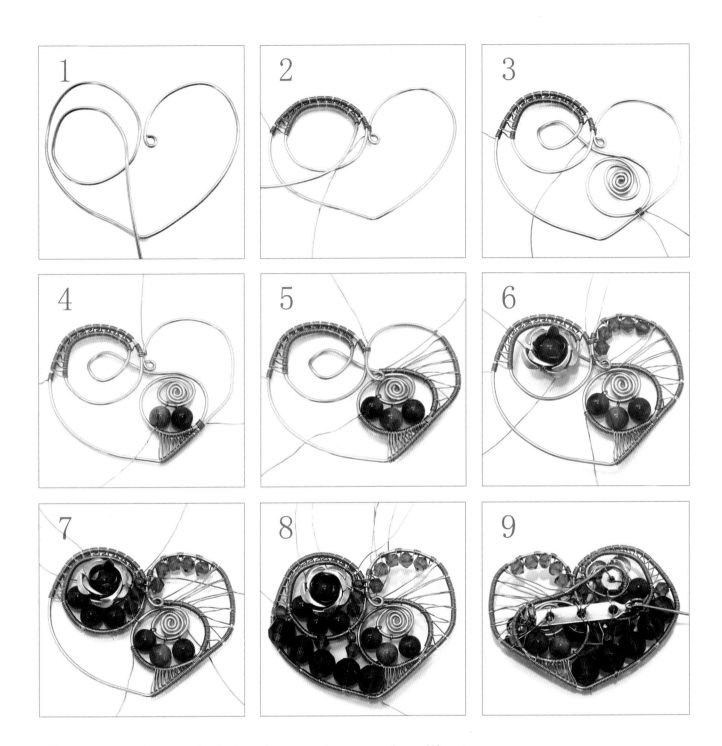

When you have finished weaving and coiling the 28-gauge wire, do not trim it until the piece is completely finished, as the ends are useful for securing the brooch pin.

Necklace

1 With round-nose pliers, grasp a 20in (500mm) piece of 18-gauge wire approx. 3½in (90mm) from the end. Bend the two sides of the wire up to form the tip of the heart shape. Bend the shorter end of the wire round the large end of a ring mandrel to form one half of the heart, and finish with a small loop. Repeat for the other side, but finish by making a concentric circle within the top of the heart.

2 Secure a 40in (1m) piece of 28-gauge copper wire by wrapping three times around the two parallel wires that form the center of the heart, leaving an 8in (200mm) tail. Begin a weave to the left-hand side of the heart, coiling six times around the outer frame (see page 18). Pass the wire over then under the parallel circle of wire and coil five times. Repeat these two steps until the weave reaches around the arc of the heart.

3 Using 18-gauge wire, form another concentric circle. Take it in an arc to the lower right side of the heart frame to form a clockwise circle. Form a decreasing spiral in the top half of this circle and trim the wire. Attach the center of an 80in (2m) length of 28-gauge wire to the heart frame and lower circle at the point where the wires meet and lie parallel.

4 Using the lower 40in (1m) of 28-gauge wire, weave three times around the frame and twice around the lower circle. End at the lower tip of the heart and finish by coiling around the circle. At the same time, add two 6mm amethyst beads within the circle at the first and last rounds of weaving. After the first round coil round the circle, take the wire through the bead, twice around the outer spiral wire, back through the bead, around the circle again, and continue the weave.

5 Still with 28-gauge wire, coil around the circle frame to the center of the remaining piece of frame wire. Add a final 6mm bead as before. Using the upper 40in (1m) of 28-gauge wire added at Step 4, weave the teardrop shape in the top right half of the heart. Coil ten times around each side until the lower wire is full. End with the wire on the outer frame.

6 Coil five times around the heart frame and add a 4mm bicone. Coil five times around the frame again. Continue adding 4mm bicones, ending by coiling five times around the frame. Attach the large metallic flower to the inner, upper circle. Center a 6mm amethyst bead on 11¾in (300mm) of 28-gauge wire and thread both ends of wire through the flower. Wrap each wire individually around the central concentric circle to secure.

7 Using the 28-gauge wire left over from Step 2, attach three amethyst beads within the outer concentric circle, coiling around the outer circle 20 times between beads. Attach two 4mm bicones and one 3mm bead in the same way, coiling 15 times between the bicones.

8 Attach a 39⅜in (1m) piece of 28-gauge wire to the lower tip of the outer frame. Following the method used to add amethyst beads in Step 4, fill the space in the lower part of the heart frame with an assortment of 8mm crystals, 4mm bicones, and 3mm beads. Coil the outer frame as you go. Any small gaps between beads will be filled later when securing the brooch pin.

9 Attach a smaller metallic flower beside the lower spiral as in Step 6, using a 3mm bead as the center. Using the remaining tails of 28-gauge wire, secure the brooch pin to the back. Place it out of sight and weave the wire around 18-gauge wire where it is least obvious on the front. Simultaneously, fill gaps with 4mm bicones and 3mm beads. Secure and trim any remaining tail wires.

Earrings

YOU WILL NEED

4 x 1in (25mm) headpins, copper

2 x earwires, copper

1 x 5in (125mm) length of US 28-gauge (SWG 30, 0.3mm) wire, copper

2 x 8mm faceted beads, amethyst

2 x 6mm beads, amethyst

8 x tiny chips, amethyst

Make these using a mixture of the beads used for the brooch. Place four beads on eyepins and make simple loops at the top (see page 15). Using 28-gauge wire, attach a few amethyst chips to the bottom of the earwires above the loops. Link all the loops together to complete the earrings.

Heart of Glass

Create this intricately woven heart pendant and complementary bracelet by Sue Mason-Burns in vibrant summer colors. The versatile wire weave enhances the natural shape of the glass heart.

FOR THE NECKLACE YOU WILL NEED

1 x reel of US 18-gauge (SWG 19, 1mm) wire, vintage bronze

1 x reel of US 28-gauge (SWG 30, 0.3mm) wire, vintage bronze

1 x 30mm glass heart bead

30 x 5mm agate beads, multicolored

8 x 8mm round faceted crystals, blue

1 x 10mm jumprings, vintage bronze

18 x 5mm jumprings, vintage bronze

Side cutters

Round-nose pliers

Chain-nose pliers

Bail-making pliers: large, medium, and small

Hammer

Steel bench block

Bracelet

YOU WILL NEED

8 x 10mm agate beads, multicolored

8 x 2in (50mm) eyepins, antique bronze

2 x 6mm jumprings, antique bronze

1 x toggle clasp, antique bronze

Make a simple bracelet with 10mm multicolored agate beads to match the chain of your necklace. Simply thread eyepins through each bead and link these together. Add a decorative toggle clasp.

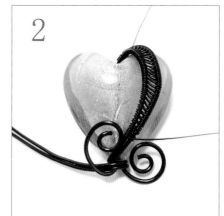

Vary the style of the necklace by adding accent beads to the weave or forming different shapes to the open spirals with the lower wires.

Necklace

1 Flush cut two 11¾in (300mm) lengths of 18-gauge wire and 59in (1.5m) of 28-gauge wire. Curve one 18-gauge wire and lay the wires parallel. Starting 4in (100mm) in and leaving an 11¾in (300mm) tail, coil 28-gauge wire three times around both wires. Where they separate, coil twice around the lower wire. Pass under the upper wire and coil three times. Repeat to where the wires meet again and coil three times round both wires.

2 Thread the two wires above the weave through the heart bead and bend them so the weave lies across one side of the heart. Wind the two remaining 18-gauge tail wires around the wires threaded through the heart. Form decorative open spirals with the threaded wires to either side of the woven section. Wind both remaining tail wires together in an arc behind one spiral and in front of the other.

3 Take the two wires across the lower part of the woven section, where one end of the 28-gauge tail wire is. Coil the tail wire five times around the two wires, trim and secure. Continue the two wires up to meet the remaining section of 28-gauge tail wire at the top of the heart. Coil this tail wire around both wires for 1¾6in (20mm)—this section will form the bail of the pendant.

4 Bend the coiled section made at Step 3 around the larger side of medium bail-making pliers. Separate the two remaining unwoven tail wires and wind each in turn around the front of the bail. Trim each wire to a length of ⅜in (10mm) and form a tight spiral at the back of the heart bead to hold the wires in place.

5 Flush cut 18 1⁹⁄₁₆in (40mm) lengths of 18-gauge wire and make a simple loop at one end of each piece (see page 15). Thread one 8mm crystal onto eight of the wire pieces and form a loop. For the rest, use three agate beads in complementary colors. Lay out your design on a design board to ensure the correct layout and length.

6 Make two equal sections of necklace chain by linking each end of the loops using 5mm jumprings (see page 14). Alternate agate sections with single crystals, beginning and ending each chain with agate sections. The number of beads you use will depend on the desired length of the chain.

7 Attach the heart focal bead using a 10mm jumpring. Use 5mm jumprings to attach each section of necklace chain to the 10mm jumpring. You could also attach directly to the bail or run a continuous necklace chain through the bail, but this method ensures that the focal heart lies flat.

8 For the clasp eye, flush cut a 2½in (60mm) piece of 18-gauge wire and bend the center around the larger side of medium bail-making pliers. Form small inward loops with each tail. For the hook, flush cut a 2¾in (70mm) length of 18-gauge wire. Form a small loop in one end, wind this end around the larger side of large bail-making pliers. Form a closed spiral with the remaining wire.

9 Hammer the clasp sections flat, then attach the clasp to the ends of the necklace sections. To attach the eye, use a 5mm jumpring through the loop of the necklace and the section of the eye where the wires cross. To attach the hook, use a 10mm jumpring and attach through the loop of the necklace and the center of the spiral.

Falling Leaves

Take a leaf from Mother Nature's book and use wire to create flowing, organic shapes. This beautiful set by Laura Binding intertwines wire-formed leaves and gemstone-wired flowers.

FOR THE NECKLACE YOU WILL NEED

1 x reel of US 26-gauge (SWG 27, 0.4mm) wire, antique bronze

1 x reel of US 22-gauge (SWG 23, 0.6mm) wire, antique bronze

1 x reel of US 18-gauge (SWG 19, 1mm) wire, antique bronze

10 x 8mm center-drilled ovals, Botswana agate

5 x large-center, drilled nuggets, amazonite

3 x rondelles, amazonite

Side cutters

Round-nose pliers

Hammer

Steel bench block

Earrings

YOU WILL NEED

1 x 39⅜in (1m) length of US 18-gauge (SWG 19, 1mm) wire, antique bronze

1 x 39⅜in (1m) length of US 22-gauge (SWG 23, 0.6mm) wire, antique bronze

2 x 6mm rondelle beads

2 x earwires, antique bronze

Create a single leaf using 18-gauge wire. Using 22-gauge wire, spiral and wrap to the leaf. Wrap around the top and add a rondelle before finishing with spirals. Add earwires to finish.

Necklace

1 Cut approx. 20in (500mm) of 18-gauge wire (depending on how large you want the flowers) and bring the tails together. Cross them over and form an oval measuring just over 2in (50mm). This will look like a little fish with the wires crossed at the top. Mold the shape until you are happy with the design. Place the pliers at the oval and twist to create a kink.

2 Reshape the oval using your fingers until it resembles a leaf. Holding the leaf by the crossed wires, place it on a steel block, and hammer the ends of the leaf hard to create a flattened look. Bring one of the crossed wires around to form another oval. Create another kink at the end, hammer, and wrap the tail around the center.

3 Repeat the shaping and hammering process with the remaining wire, then bring it to the middle and wrap. When the shape is secure, cut any excess wire short to prevent sharp edges touching the skin. Repeat steps 1–3 but form smaller ovals of around 1in (35mm). Make three sets of both sizes in total.

4 Cut around 16in (400mm) of 26-gauge wire. Add the first oval bead and bring it to the middle of the wire. Take the wire down the back of the bead and twist it together with the wire emerging from the bead. Twist twice before adding the second bead. Repeat five times, then add a rondelle and bring it across the center.

5 Stack the two leaves and flowers together. Using the wire from the flower, bind them together by wrapping around all the pieces. Repeat with the other two sets and arrange the three pieces together. Using the wire from the flowers, you will be able to wrap the leaves together behind the flower so the wire is not visible but the components become one solid piece.

6 Cut two 9½in (240mm) pieces of 18-gauge wire and create a large (approx. ½in/6mm) wrapped loop (see page 16) at one end on each piece. Add a rondelle, then coil this wire using 22-gauge wire for 4⅜in (110mm). Add another rondelle and create another wrapped loop at the end, attaching it to the focal leaves piece (at Step 7 of the wrapped loop technique on page 16) before you close the loop. Place the other piece on the opposite side of the focal leaves. Flatten one end loop into a hook shape to create the clasp.

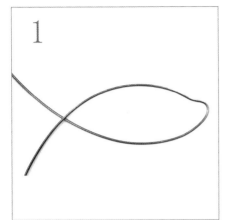

1

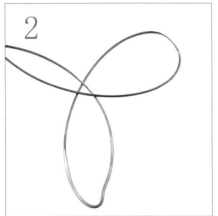

2

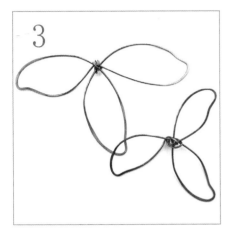

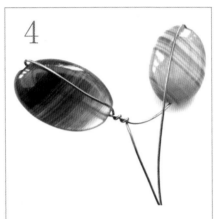

3

4

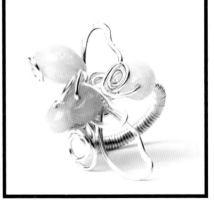

5

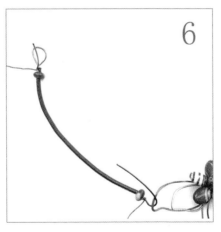

6

Ring

YOU WILL NEED

1 x 20in (510mm) length
of US 18-gauge (SWG 19,
1mm) wire, silver-colored

1 x 10in (255mm) length
of US 22-gauge (SWG 23,
0.6mm) wire, silver-colored

4 x 6–10mm semiprecious
gem beads

Ring mandrel

Cut the 18-gauge wire in half
and place the sections together.
Wrap the 22-gauge wire tightly
around the 18-gauge wires for
approx. 1½in/30mm). Bend
this coiled section around the
mandrel. Make leaf shapes at the
ends of the 18-gauge wire, adding
the beads on in a random pattern.
Finish each wire with a coil or
tuck the cut ends into the middle
of the beaded piece.

When hammering, make sure you hold
the piece at the edge of the steel block
and strike at the center to ensure
you avoid hitting your fingers.

Ocean Waves

Transport yourself to a peaceful beach with this freeform wirework necklace and pretty earrings by Hilary Sahota. Silvery links interspaced with blue gemstones evoke white surf and gentle waves under a cloudless sky.

FOR THE NECKLACE YOU WILL NEED

1 x 13–16½ft (4–5m) length of US 26-gauge (SWG 27, 0.4mm) wire, silver-plated

7 x 6in (150mm) lengths of US 20-gauge (SWG 21, 0.8mm) wire, silver-plated (for wave links)

8 x 1³⁄₁₆in lengths (30mm) of US 20-gauge (SWG 21, 0.8mm) wire, silver-plated (for beaded link)

1 x 3¼in (80mm) length of US 16-gauge (SWG 18, 1.25mm) wire (for clasp)

8 x 10mm coin beads

12–14 x 4mm beads

12–14 x rice pearls

1 x clasp of your choice

1 x 6mm jumpring

Round-nose pliers

Flat-nose pliers

Side cutters

Earrings

YOU WILL NEED

2 x 10mm agate coin beads, blue sponge

2 x 6mm rice pearls

2 x 2in (50mm) ball-ended headpins, silver-colored

2 x 2in (50mm) eyepins, silver-colored

2 x earwires, silver-colored

Attach a coin-bead link to a simple shepherd's hook ear wire and add a wrapped-loop pearl drop, for a simple but elegant pair of earrings.

Necklace

1 Bend a 6in (150mm) length of wire in half around round-nose pliers to make a loop. Twist the loop once. Starting next to this loop, make freeform bends with one "arm" of the wire using the round-nose pliers, leaving 1–1³⁄₁₆in (25–30mm) at the end.

2 Repeat the freeform bends on the other "arm" of the wire. Bend one end into a loop with a 1–1³⁄₁₆in (25–30mm) tail.

3 Wrap the first tail end around this loop to close the link and secure it. Wrap the other tail end around the loop. Cut off any excess wire and press down firmly with the flat-nose pliers so that any wire ends are flush with the piece.

4 Cut off around 23⅝in (600mm) of 26-gauge wire. Starting at one loop end of the frame and leaving 1³⁄₁₆in (30mm) of wire to hold on to, wrap the long end twice around one side of the frame. Bring the wire up through the middle, over to the other side, and wrap around twice. Repeat to form a figure-of-eight wrap that crosses in the middle of the frame.

5 Continue wrapping until you have covered about two-thirds of the frame. Make two tight wraps and cut off the wire, pressing down firmly with pliers. Beginning at the opposite end and using 11¾in (300mm) of 26-gauge wire, start wrapping as before, but thread on a 4mm bead or pearl. Wrap the wire a couple of times and add more beads to fill the gap.

6 Wrap the wire tightly a couple of times and cut off the end. Neaten any tails or ends that you may have left sticking out. Repeat to make seven wave links.

7 Make a loop at one end of the 1³⁄₁₆in (30mm) wire. Add a coin bead, bend the wire down against the bead. Trim if necessary before making a loop. Repeat to make eight beaded loops (see page 15).

8 Assemble the links, alternating the wave link and the coin bead link.

9 Add a clasp or make a simple hook. For an "S"-shape clasp cut a 2in (50mm) piece of 16-gauge wire and bend each end into a small loop with round-nose pliers. Using the widest part of the round-nose pliers, curve the piece into an "S" shape as shown.

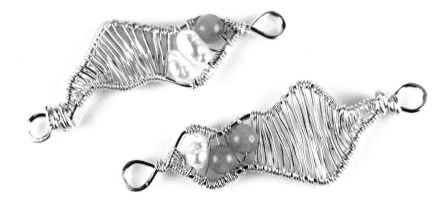

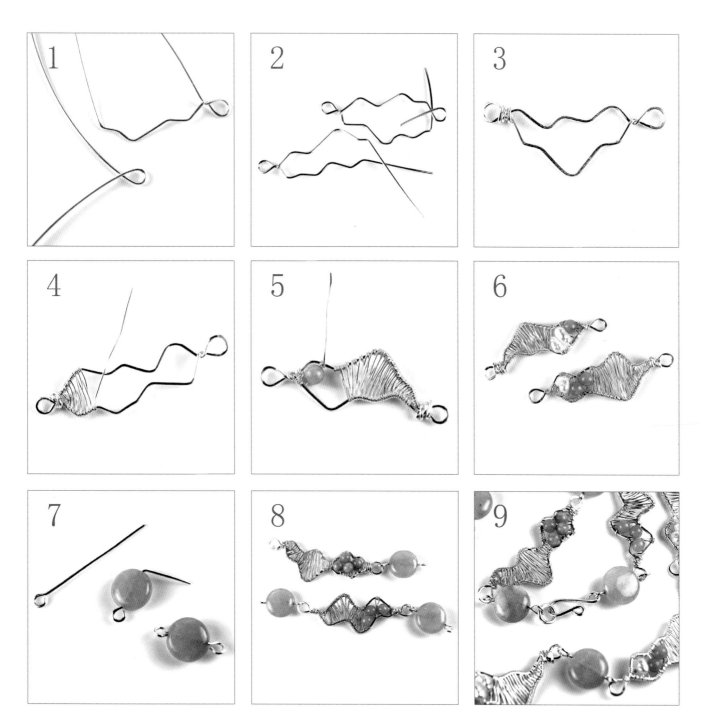

Freeform woven links are great if you have trouble making identical components in your jewelry!

Let's Twist

Give traditional macramé a funky wire twist with this striking design by Sue Mason-Burns for a bracelet and earrings. Choose beads in vibrant colors that will make the bright copper tones of the wire "pop".

FOR THE BRACELET YOU WILL NEED

1 x reel of US 14-gauge (SWG 16, 1.5mm) wire, non-tarnish copper

1 x reel of US 20-gauge (SWG 21, 0.8mm) wire, non-tarnish copper

1 x reel of US 20-gauge (SWG 21, 0.8mm) wire, half-round, copper

Selection of large-hole lampwork beads

Wooden ring vice

Medium bail-making pliers

Flat-nose pliers

Side cutters

Chasing hammer

Steel bench block

Bracelet-forming pliers (optional)

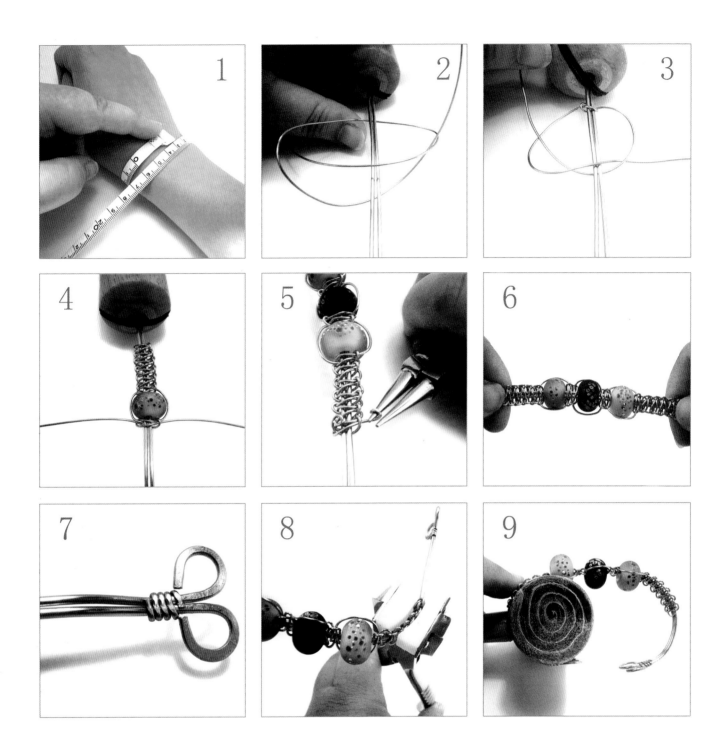

This design also works beautifully as a torque bangle style, with a single central wire in a thicker gauge.

Necklace

1 Measure your wrist to find the size for your bangle, and add a further 2½in (60mm) to allow for the loops at the ends of the central wires and give space on your wrist for it to move. If you prefer a looser fit, add a little more. Flush cut two lengths of 14-gauge wire to this measurement (see page 20).

2 Flush cut 39in (1m) of 20-gauge wire. Clamp the two lengths of 14-gauge wire parallel in the end of a ring vice. Centre the 20-gauge wire behind these wires, 2¾in (70mm) from the clamped end. Lay the right-hand end over the two central wires, forming a "D" shape. Pass the left-hand end over the right-hand wire, under the central wires, and up through the "D" shape. Pull wires firmly to complete the knot.

3 Repeat with the left-hand side of the wire. Lay it across the two central wires, passing the right-hand wire over the left-hand wire, under the central wires, and up through the "D" shape. Pull the knot tight.

4 Repeat these knots, alternating the starting wire, until the knotted section is approximately 1in (25mm), or 12 knots long. Slide a bead along both central wires until the bead reaches the knotted section. Bring both sides of the 20-gauge wire around the sides of the bead, forming a frame on either side of the bead. Continue knotting as before on the other side of the bead.

5 Make three knots after the bead added in Step 4 and add another bead. Continue knotting after the bead as in Step 4. Make three further knots and add the final bead. After the final bead, make a knotted section the same length as the section before the addition of the first bead. Trim and finish the 20-gauge wires with small spirals. Secure these inside the bangle.

6 Unclamp the central wires from the ring vice. The knotted sections and beads will still slide along these central wires, so now is the time to make sure your bangle design is central on the wires. When you are happy with the look, grasp the two outer knotted sections and push them firmly toward the center. This will neaten the appearance of the knots.

7 Using the larger jaw of medium bail-making pliers, turn simple outward loops to each end of the central wires. Use a hammer and steel bench block to hammer these loops flat. Flush cut two 2in (50mm) lengths of half-round wire and wrap around the two central wires four times, just below the loops at each end of the bangle. Trim and secure with flat-nose pliers.

8 Use bracelet-forming pliers, if you have them, to gently shape the bangle. Beginning at the outer sections of knotted wire, gently clamp within the pliers and shape. Move the pliers along the length of the bangle. Repeat for the opposite side. The finished bangle should be oval rather than circular.

9 If you do not have bracelet-forming pliers, use a cylindrical object approximately 1³⁄₁₆in (30mm) in diameter (such as a rawhide mallet) to form each side of the bangle shape. Position the mandrel off-center on each side of the bangle, and wrap around the "arms" of the bangle. Repeat for the opposite side.

Earrings

YOU WILL NEED

2 x earwires, copper

6 x small Lucite flower beads

6 x 1in (25mm) eyepins, copper

6 x 6mm jumprings, copper

2 x 1½in (40mm) lengths of US 14-gauge (SWG 16, 1.5mm) wire, copper

2 x 20in (510mm) lengths of US 20-gauge (SWG 21, 0.8mm) wire, copper

Turn a loop at each end of a single central wire to whatever length you require. Use the knotting technique from the bangle to fill the space between the loops on your central wire. Hang earwires from the loop at one end and either a single bead or a cluster of beads in complementary colors from the lower loop.

Festive Berries

Get into the festive spirit with this sensational clover link collection by Hilary Sahota. Sparkling silver is decked with berry-like crystals for a knockout party set.

FOR THE NECKLACE YOU WILL NEED

1 x 79in (2m) length of US 18-gauge (SWG 19, 1mm) wire, silver-plated

44 x 3.5mm jumprings, silver-plated

6 x 6mm crystal beads, red

5 x 4mm crystal beads, red

5 x 10mm crystal beads, red

17 x 3mm beads, silver-plated

Round-nose pliers

Snipe-nose pliers

Side cutters

Steel block

Hammer

Necklace

1 Using approx. 2¾–3½in (70–90mm) of wire, form a loop with round-nose pliers to make the clover link. Make a second loop the same size, next to the first. Make a third loop at right angles to the last and bring the wire up parallel to the original loop. Make the fourth loop next to the last and trim off the tail.

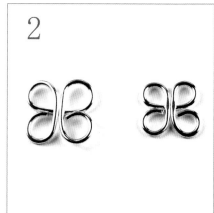

2 Flatten the link gently with a hammer and block. Make 5 larger links and 14 of the smaller links. For a longer necklace, add more links.

3 Attach clover links for the necklace elements using two jumprings. The double jumpring adds strength as well as being a nice design element.

4 Make simple drops using a headpin, or make your own by flattening the end of the wire with a hammer. Thread on a small silver bead, a 10mm bead, a 4mm bead, then turn a loop at the end (see page 15). Join to the large clover links.

5 Make an eyepin and thread on a small silver bead, a 6mm bead, another small silver bead, then turn another loop. Interspace these eyepins with the small clover links to make the "chain" part of your necklace.

6 Finish with a standard clasp or make a simple hook clasp. Using 18-gauge wire, cut a 2in (50mm) length and bead into a large "U" shape. Form simple loops at both ends, making one loop as small as possible and the other big enough to attach to one end of the necklace. Add a large jumpring to the other end as the catch for the hook.

To turn this necklace into something even more special, use real pearls.

Try working directly from the roll or spool of wire, rather than cutting off measured sections for the clover link. This should cut down on wastage.

Bracelet

YOU WILL NEED

7 x 6mm crystal beads, red

7 x 1in (25mm) eyepins, silver-colored

52 x 4mm jumprings, silver-colored

1 x 78in (2m) length of US-18 gauge (SWG 19, 1mm) wire, silver-colored

The matching bracelet takes the linking design one stage further. For a more substantial bracelet, use the clover link in groups of four, interlinked with beaded eyepins. To make a wider bracelet, increase the number of clover links widthways to three or even four and leave out the beads for a chic, contemporary look.

Earrings

YOU WILL NEED

2 x 10mm crystal beads, red

2 x 4mm crystal beads, red

2 x 2in (50mm) headpins, silver-colored

2 x 3in (75mm) lengths of US 18-gauge (SWG 19, 1mm) wire, silver-colored

2 x earwires, silver-colored

A simple pair of earrings can be made with the clover link and a matching drop, attached to shepherd's hook earwires.

Quetzalcoatl

Invoke the Aztec feathered serpent Quetzalcoatl—the god of arts, crafts, and knowledge—with these fabulous feathered earrings and pendant designed by James Ferris. Explore the imagery of this fascinating culture by using intricate spirals and bold colors.

FOR THE EARRINGS YOU WILL NEED

1 x reel of US 18-gauge (SWG 19, 1mm) wire

1 x reel of US 20-gauge (SWG 21, 0.8mm) wire

1 x reel of US 24-gauge (SWG 25, 0.5mm) wire

1 x selection of colored guinea fowl feathers (red and blue)

4 x beads to match color of feathers, such as red coral and turquoise

2 x flat disc beads of about 18mm diameter and about 5mm thick (howlite)

2 x earhook wires

Side cutters

Chain-nose pliers

Round-nose pliers

Round multi-mandrel

Liver of sulfur (if using copper wire)

Rubber gloves (if using copper wire)

Safety goggles (if using copper wire)

Fine wire wool (if using copper wire)

Pendant

YOU WILL NEED

1 x 20in (510mm) length of US 18-gauge (SWG 19, 1mm) wire, copper

1 x 12in (300mm) length of US 20-gauge (SWG 21, 0.8mm) wire, copper

1 x 31½in (800mm) length of US 24-gauge (SWG 25, 0.5mm) wire, copper

1 x 8mm jumpring, copper

1 x 18mm flat, disc bead

6 x 10mm donut beads, red and turquoise

4 x guinea fowl feathers, red and turquoise

1 x ribbon and cord finished necklace

Make a single earring piece by following the main steps and add to a larger frame. For the frame, cut 11¾in (300mm) of 18-gauge wire. Make the center small loop first, and measure ⅝in (15mm) either side to make the others. Using the round mandrel, form around the second size down from the handle.

1

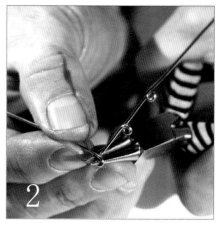

2

4

5

7

8

Try out different mandrel shapes, such as a square or triangle, for the frame.

Earrings

1 Working from left to right, cut 8¼in (210mm) of 18-gauge wire. Make a mark on it at 2½in (60mm), 3in (75mm), and 4in (100mm). Also mark the round-nose pliers, 3⁄16in (5mm) down from the tip.

2 Starting at the 2½in (60mm) mark, make a loop following the mark on the pliers. For the first loop, fold the short end of the wire counterclockwise round the pliers, then at the second and third mark wind clockwise using the longer end of the wire. The design is enhanced if the earrings mirror each other, so carry out each stage twice to make the pair.

3 Cut two 8in (200mm) lengths of 24-gauge wire, then start wrapping the wire in between the three loops you have made.

4 Bend the wire frame round the fifth size from the handle of the round multi-mandrel. Make the short end of the wire the neck for the eyeloop, then wrap the long end of the wire round the neck twice.

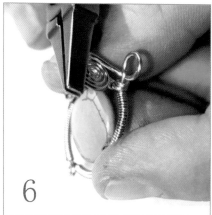

5 Cut 15¾in (400mm) of 24-gauge wire. Starting at one end of the wire, wrap from the neck down to the middle loop. Place the flat disc bead on the wire, cross over to the other side, then wrap back up to the neck.

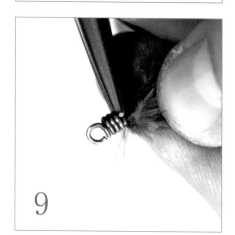

6 Create an eyeloop that faces you, out of the neck. Cut the arm to 2¾in (70mm) and create a spiral. Hammer the eye loop and the spiral to work-harden the wire. Repeat, reversing the direction of the spiral, for the second earring.

7 Cut about 11¾in (300mm) of 20-gauge wire to attach the feathers. Following the mark on the round-nose pliers, make four springs of six or seven loops each. Using the chain-nose pliers, turn up the top loop to create an eye.

8 Cut two lengths of 20-gauge wire at 3¼in (80mm) and make an eye on each. Thread on the beads and fold the wire to the left for one earring and the right for the other. Trim the wire to 2in (50mm), create spirals, then hammer. If you are using copper, patinate components with liver of sulfur and buff and polish with fine wire wool and a good polishing cloth (see page 21) before assembling.

9 Attach the feathers by inserting the ends in the eyeloop springs and gently crimping the end loop around them. Assemble the earrings, placing the feathers on the outside loops of the frames and the beaded headpins on the center loops.

Indian Spice

Be inspired by Eastern style with this beautiful set by Sian Hamilton, which combines glorious gold and regal red for an opulent look.

FOR THE NECKLACE YOU WILL NEED

1 x reel of US 18-gauge (SWG 19, 1mm) wire, gold-plated

1 x reel of US 20-gauge (SWG 21, 0.8mm) wire, gold-plated

1 x reel of US 24-gauge (SWG 25, 0.5mm) wire, gold-plated

13 x 8mm fire-polished beads

42 x 4mm fire-polished beads

Round-nose pliers

Flat-nose or chain-nose pliers

Side cutters

Hammer

Steel block

In step 7 you'll find the curved wires tend to spring off the pin. Use your free hand to hold them tightly, pulling them down slightly and keeping them under tension as you create the loop at the end of the pin.

Necklace

1 To make the chain, take the roll of 20-gauge wire and thread on a fire-polished 8mm bead. Push it up the wire to keep it out of the way. Make a simple loop on the end of the wire (see page 15). Wrap 24-gauge wire about seven times around the 20-gauge wire and cut off. Push the bead down to the coil and make another coil after the bead. Finish with another simple loop and cut off the roll.

2 Following Step 1, make ten beaded sections using 4mm fire-polished beads. You could use the same seven coil wraps and two 4mm beads per section. Take the two different types of chain sections and make two chains, alternating the sections with 4mm jumprings in between. Finish the ends with 8mm beads and a jumpring.

3 To make the pendant section, take a 3¼in (80mm) length of 18-gauge wire and flatten one end with a hammer. The end must be wide enough to stop an 8mm bead falling off. Set aside ready for Step 5.

4 Cut four lengths of 18-gauge wire: 4in (100mm), 3¼in (80mm), 2¾in (70mm), and 2½in (60mm). Make simple loops at both ends and curve all four pieces—a pencil sharpener holder can be used to do this. The loops on the ends must be at a right angle to the curve, so that you can feed them onto the straight pin with the curves facing out each side.

5 To check the fit, place the beads and curved wires on the pin in this order: 8mm bead; bottom loop of 4in (100mm) curve; 8mm bead; bottom loop of 3¼in (80mm) curve; bottom loop of 2¾in (70mm) curve; 8mm bead; bottom loop of 2½in (60mm) curve; top loop of 2¾in (70mm) curve; top loop of 2½in (60mm) curve; top loop of 4in (100mm) curve, and the top loop of the 3¼in (80mm) curve. Adjust the wires so they all sit flat together.

6 Remove the curved wires from the pin. Wrap 24-gauge wire around the 4in (100mm) curve three times at one end. Add a 4mm bead, wrap the wire twice around the curve, then add another bead. Continue in this way, adding a bead to every third wrap. Repeat for the 3¼in (80mm) curve. Leave the 2¾in (70mm) curve undecorated. Wrap the 2½in (60mm) curve completely in 24-gauge wire.

7 Feed all the curves back onto the pin exactly as in Step 5. Make another loop at the end of the pin, feed on a 4mm jumpring, and add an 8mm jumpring.

8 To join the final sections, take another length of 24-gauge wire and wrap a few times around the 2¾in (70mm) wire. This will be the inner left-hand wire as you look at the pendant. Using the main image for guidance, wrap once around the outer wire underneath the bead and again twice around the inner wire. Repeat, making sure the wire goes under the bead on the outer wire. Repeat for the other side.

9 To make the clasp, take a 4in (100mm) length of 18-gauge wire and curve into a loop. Spiral one end and make a simple loop at the other. Take the chains from Step 2 and attach the 4mm jumpring ends to the 8mm ring on the pendant piece. Attach another 8mm jumpring to one chain and the clasp section to the other end to finish.

Earrings

YOU WILL NEED

1 x 5½in (140mm) length of US 18-gauge (SWG 19, 1mm) wire, gold-colored

1 x 5½in (140mm) length of US 20-gauge (SWG 21, 0.8mm) wire, gold-colored

1 x 16in (400mm) length of US 24-gauge (SWG 25, 0.5mm) wire, gold-colored

2 x 8mm faceted bead, red

8 x 6mm faceted bead, red

2 x earwires, gold-colored

Make a 2¾in (70mm) pin with a hammered end. Feed on an 8mm bead and coil with 24-gauge wire, leaving approx. ⅜in (100mm) at the end plain. Cut two 2¾in (70mm) pieces of 20-gauge wire and make a loop at one end on both pieces. Curve both into semi-circles. Feed four 6mm beads onto one curved wire and make a loop at the open end. Feed one loop on the beaded curve onto the plain curved wire and make a loop at the open end, trapping the beaded curve. Feed the plain curved piece onto the pin, making sure the loops are large enough to go over the coiled section of the pin. Add the top loop of the beaded curve to the pin and close the pin with a loop. Add an earwire to the top and repeat to make a pair.

It's a Wrap

This delicate wire embellishment technique by James Ferris is a simple yet ingenious way to add interest to beads, but looks equally stunning used alone.

FOR THE PENDANT YOU WILL NEED

1 x reel of US 18-gauge (SWG 19, 1mm) wire

1 x reel of US 20-gauge (SWG 21, 0.8mm) wire

1 x reel of US 28-gauge (SWG 30, 0.3mm) wire

1 x 20mm bead

1 x 15mm bead

1 x 10mm bead

Masking tape

Side cutters

Hand drill (optional)

Ring

YOU WILL NEED

1 x 8in (200mm) length of US 16-gauge (SWG 18, 1.25mm) wire, copper

1 x 83in (2.1m) length of US 28-gauge (SWG 30, 0.3mm) wire, copper

Follow Steps 1–7 using two 16-gauge wires at 4in (100m) or 4⅓in (110mm) depending on the ring size, and 83in (2.1m) of 28-gauge wire for the weaving.

Earrings

YOU WILL NEED

1 x 16in (405mm) length of US 20-gauge (SWG 21, 0.8mm) wire, copper

1 x 43in (1.1m) length of US 28-gauge (SWG 30, 0.3mm) wire, copper

2 x 15mm beads

2 x earwires, copper

Follow steps 1–7 and use any of the measurements supplied to suit the size of your beads.

Pendant

1 For the 20mm bead, flush-cut two 4in (100mm) pieces of 18-gauge wire, taping the two wires together at one end so they are the same. Cut 70in (1.8m) of the 28-gauge wire and fold it in half. Starting from the middle of the two 18-gauge wires and the center of the 28-gauge wire, start a figure-of-eight weave (round once, round twice cross over).

2 Weave down one side of the two 18-gauge wires until you have 1in (25mm) of bare wire at the end.

3 Make a loop in the end of one of the wires big enough for a 1mm eyepin to go through. With the other piece, create a loose spiral (see page 17 for technique, but don't make it tight), until you reach halfway between the loop and the weave. Bend the two wires out slightly in a small "V" shape.

4 Carry on weaving down toward the spiral until you cannot weave neatly any further. Wrap the remaining wire down to the loop and trim off. Using the flat-nose pliers slightly spiral the loop in, but make this much less than for the other spiral.

5 Remove the tape and repeat for the other side following Steps 2–4, but making sure the loop and spiral are on opposite sides. This is very important, or the design will not work.

6 Cut about 3¼in (80mm) of 18-gauge wire, make a large loop at one end and set aside. For the 15mm and 10mm bead, make the loops small. Place the center of the finished weave over the bead. Start bending the ends around your bead to hug it, ending up with the two spirals facing each other at a slight angle.

7 With the loop end of the weave, slowly mold them over the bead until they are in line with the holes. Place the eyepin (made in Step 6) through and make a smaller eye to lock the weave in place. Now take your time, slowly molding and shaping the weave to the bead. Use the flat-nose pliers to tighten up the loop with the eyepin through it.

8 Repeat Steps 1–7. For the 15mm bead, use two 2¾in (70mm) lengths of 20-gauge wire and 43in (1.1m) of 28-gauge wire for the weaving, leaving 1in (25mm) bare at the ends for the spiral and loop. For the 10mm bead, use two 2½in (60mm) lengths of 20-gauge wire and 28in (700mm) of 28-gauge, leaving about ¾in (18mm) bare at the ends. Make a spiral headpin for the small bead using the directions in Step 3.

9 Join them together, making sure the large loop in the big bead is on top. Create a twisted large jumpring for the large loop by twisting 20-gauge in a handheld drill. Cut about 15¾in (400mm) of 20-gauge wire and fold in half. Place the two ends in the drill chuck. Hold a pen in the other end and start up. If you want the finished piece to have a darkened antique look then use liver of sulfur to patinate (see page 21).

Try using a variety of colored wires to create a range of effects.

Wire & Swirls

Drawing inspiration from ironwork in the beautiful city of Paris, this stunning necklace and earrings set by Sian Hamilton will ensure you stand out from the crowd.

FOR THE NECKLACE YOU WILL NEED

Approx. 160in (4m) of US 18-gauge (SWG 19, 1mm) wire, copper

1 x 780in (20m) length of US 26-gauge (SWG 28, 0.4mm) wire, copper

76 x 2.5mm (size 8) seed beads: in silver-lined turquoise, multi iris, and dark amethyst

1 x 8in (200mm) length of US 20-gauge (SWG 21, 0.8mm) wire

4 x 6mm x 4mm oval jumprings

1 x clasp

1 x chain (of choice)

Round-nose pliers

Side cutters

Necklace

1 Take a piece of paper and scribble a few lines on it—let your imagination run free. You'll see from the sketch in the picture that the final design isn't exactly what was sketched but it was a start to get the design going. To copy this design exactly use the main image as a template.

2 With the roll of 18-gauge wire, begin making your drawn shapes. Using round-nose pliers, curve the wire, laying it over the drawn shape to check. If you can't draw, just lay the wire over the image on page 70. When you are happy with the shapes, snip them off the roll using side cutters. This design has three main "S" shape curves (the largest in the center) and three "C" shape curves that sit inside them. Keep all the curves in pairs so you know which ones go together.

3 Make up all the wire sections you need. If you are copying this design, you should end up with three main pieces and three smaller pieces. If you have a steel block and rawhide mallet, hammer them slightly to flatten and work-harden them, which helps to maintain the shape.

4 Starting with one of the smaller "S" shapes, take a length of 26-gauge wire and wrap it around the top curve. Coil about ten times—keep it about ³⁄₁₆in (5mm) away from the very end. Now start adding in beads on the outside of the "S". Add a bead, wrap around the wire twice then add another bead. Keep going until you have covered the whole of the outside top curve.

5 If you still have a good length of 26-gauge wire on the "S" then start the next weaving section with this; if not then coil the wire a couple of times and snip off. Start with the next piece of 26-gauge by coiling a couple of times. Add in the "C" shape made earlier to fit with this "S". Hold on to both wires with one hand and wrap the 26-gauge wire around both wires five times.

6 Next coil around the inside wire only, three times. Bring the 26-gauge wire over the inside wire and tuck under the "S" shape. Coil four times and bring the wire over the "S" and under the inside wire. Coil three times again. Repeat, increasing the amount of times you coil around the "S" shape as the design curves. Push the coils tightly together to reveal the crisscross pattern.

7 Weave as much of the "S" as you like. The example finishes just before the inside wire curled at the end. Coil the 26-gauge wire around the inside wire about ten times. Finally, to finish the "S" pull the lower curled end of the main "S" shape forward to give a 3D effect to this end. The inside curled end should sit behind it.

8 Use Steps 4–7 to make up the other two "S" shapes—the center main one uses the same technique, with just a longer section of curve beaded. In the example, the beading has been kept on the inside of the curve so it does not interfere with the outer sections when they are added. To achieve this, bring the beaded section in front of the "S" as you bead down.

9 Using oval jumprings, attach the three pieces together at points where they sit comfortably. You may need to wiggle the wires around to make the jumprings fit. Finally, make up two beaded wrapped-loop pieces (see page 15) with 20-gauge wire on chains to hang the wirework feature on (see main image) and, to finish, dip the whole necklace in liver of sulfur to antique the metal.

2

3

Earrings

YOU WILL NEED

2 x 4¾in (120mm) lengths of US 18-gauge (SWG 19, 1mm) wire, copper

2 x 9in (225mm) lengths of US 26-gauge (SWG 27, 0.4mm) wire, copper

12 x 2.5mm (size 8) seed beads

4 x 5mm jumprings, copper

2 x earwires, copper

Make matching earrings by using the same steps to create an identical pair of "S" shapes to hang from earwires.

5

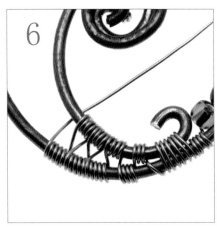

6

8

9

You can never bend the very end of a curl right round, so you always end up with a small section that is straight. To solve this, just snip off the tip after you have made the curl.

Deco Delight

Drawn from the elegant 1920s Art Deco era, this dramatic set by Sue Mason-Burns incorporates a simple weaving technique to achieve bold geometric detail.

FOR THE EARRINGS YOU WILL NEED

1 x reel of US 20-gauge (SWG 21, 0.8mm) wire

1 x reel of US 26-gauge (SWG 27, 0.4mm) wire

2 x 20mm triangle beads

2 x 6mm black jumprings

Side cutters

Medium and small bail-making pliers

Flat-nose pliers

Round-nose pliers

Chain-nose pliers

Rawhide mallet

Steel bench block

Ring mandrel

Pendant

YOU WILL NEED

2 x 8in (200mm) lengths of US 20-gauge (SWG 21, 0.8mm) wire

1 x 24in (600mm) length of US 26-gauge (SWG 27, 0.4mm) wire

1 x 20mm triangle bead

1 x 8mm jumpring, antique copper

1 x ready-made chain, antique copper

Follow the main steps to make one earring and hang it from a jumpring on a matching chain. This variation is made in copper and coated with a patina ink in age-bronze and finished with a glaze to seal.

Earrings

1   Flush cut two 8in (200mm) lengths of 20-gauge wire and one 23⅝in (600mm) length of 26-gauge wire (see page 20). Hold the frame wires parallel and begin a weave 4in (100mm) from one end, as follows: Coil three times around the lower wire, then three times around both wires. Repeat until the woven section is 1³/₁₉in (30mm) long.

2   Center the woven section of the frame wires on a ring mandrel and gently bend around until the woven section forms a semi-circular shape. Ensure that the fully coiled wire is on the inner side of the semicircle.

3   Bend the inner tail wires around the small jaw of small bail-making pliers to make a series of three loops to either side of the semicircle. End with the tail wires parallel to each other at the center of the woven section of wires.

4   Trim the tail 26-gauge wires at each end of the woven section and secure by pressing firmly against the frame wires with flat-nose pliers. Create large central loops with the larger jaw of medium bail-making pliers in the remaining 20-gauge frame wires.

5   Thread one of the tail wires from the large loops through a bead. Next, coil the remaining wire twice around the upper portion of the tail wire that was threaded through the bead, take the wire to the back of the bead, trim to around ⅝in (15mm), and form a small closed spiral to finish.

6   Trim the lower wire below the bead to around 1³/₁₉in (20mm). Form a decorative open spiral with round-nose pliers and hammer this section flat. Bend the spiral up to sit at the apex of the triangle. Trim the tail wires at the end of the upper looped section to ⅜in (10mm) long and form small loops to finish.

7   To make earwires, flush cut a 3¼in (80mm) length of 20-gauge wire. Turn a loop in one end, then bend the remaining wire around a ring mandrel to the desired size. You can make oversized earwires for this design, but you may prefer a smaller size.

8   Trim the tips of the earwires to the desired length with side cutters and make a slight bend with flat-nose pliers. Hammer the earwires with a rawhide mallet on a steel bench block to work-harden them.

9   Use 6mm jumprings to attach the earwires to the earrings around the section above the large loops at the top of the design, where one 20-gauge wire is coiled around the other. Repeat Steps 1–9 for the second earring.

Use bail-making pliers for loops rather than round-nose pliers so that you get identical-sized loops every time.

To avoid tool marks, use
a rawhide mallet when
hammering coated wire.

Tree of Life

A symbol of energy, balance, and wellbeing, this pretty tree of life by James Ferris is awash with rainbow colors, making it perfect for summer.

FOR THE PENDANT YOU WILL NEED

1 x reel of US 14-gauge (SWG 16, 1.5mm) wire

1 x reel of US 24-gauge (SWG 25, 0.5mm) wire

Selection of beads, 2mm, 3mm, 5mm in size, rainbow colors

1 x flat, round bead, about 18mm in diameter

1³⁄₁₆in (45mm) diameter mandrel

Flat-nose pliers

Side cutters

Pendant

1 Cut one 11¾in (300mm) length of 14-gauge wire and 11 pieces of 24-gauge wire 11¾in (300mm) long. Attach all the 24-gauge wire to the frame wire. To do this, fold a length of 24-gauge wire in half, place over the center of the 14-gauge, and wrap around once so the two ends face the same way. Use pliers to pinch the wraps together to neaten them.

2 To make the neck of the frame, turn one end of the 14-gauge wire at a right angle 1¾in (45mm) from the end. Using a round mandrel 1¹³⁄₁₆in (45mm) in diameter, for example a section of a rolling pin, bend the wire all the way round, making sure the neck is upright. Using flat-nose pliers, wrap the other end tightly around the neck twice.

3 Bunch the 24-gauge wire together at the base of the frame. Place the flat-nose pliers about 1⅛in (30mm) down on your bunch of wire and start twisting until the trunk is tight. Don't grip the wire too hard with the pliers. Remember which way you twisted the trunk, as you will need to follow this direction for the rest of the tree.

4 Place a sharp right-hand bend at the base of the trunk and another at the top where the twist ends to the left. Separate five wires from the main bunch to the right and twist a couple of times to the length of about ³⁄₁₆in (4mm). Give the main trunk one more twist. Note that the place where you hold the wire with your pliers when twisting is where the twist will end.

5 Separate off five wires, twist a couple of times, then give the main trunk another twist. Split the rest of the wires in the main trunk. Pull one wire out the back of the frame for the flat, round, moon bead. Twist the two remaining bunches a couple of times.

6 Place the moon bead on the wire that sticks out the back. Finish off the remaining branches by splitting and twisting again. Make sure some branches are positioned over the moon. Stylize the tree by giving the branches a few kinks, which helps to pull the wire back and leave room for the beads.

7 To attach the moon, take the wire it sits on and line it up with one of the branches. Wrap it around the branch three times and trim. If you want the moon close to the edge, attach the wire to the frame. Make sure some branches are positioned over the moon, as this keeps it steady.

8 Make sure there are ten branches on one side and 11 on the other. Start adding the beads from right to left (blue first, then green, yellow, orange, red, pink, and purple). Use three branches per color, attaching each wire as you go by wrapping it round the outside of the frame three times and trimming it off neatly.

9 Complete by using the neck wire to create a wrapped loop (see page 16) in your chosen size. Normally, the frame wire sticking out to the side would be trimmed to 1⅝in (40mm) and a loose spiral would be made to sit top center. This design looked better and the colors were shown off more effectively by omitting this step.

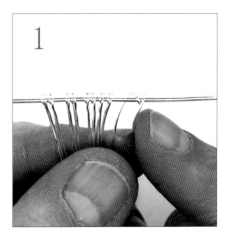

Try using metal beads of 1mm, 2mm, 3mm, and 4mm for a different effect.

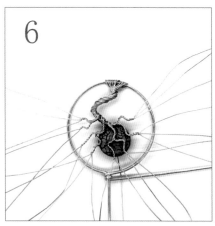

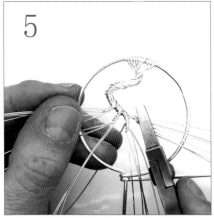

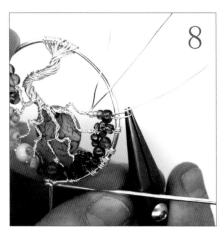

This design also suits a minimalistic approach, using just the moon bead.

Earrings

YOU WILL NEED

100 x 1.8mm (size 11) seed beads, rainbow-colored

2 x 6in (150mm) lengths of US 16-gauge (SWG 18, 1.25mm) wire, silver-colored

20 x 7in (180m) lengths of US 28-gauge (SWG 30, 0.3mm) wire, silver-colored

2 x earwires, silver-colored

Follow all the main steps, using 6in (150mm) of 16-gauge wire for the frame, 10 lengths of 28-gauge wire at 7in (180mm) for the tree, 1.8mm (size 11) seed beads, and a mandrel of 1in (25mm) diameter for the frame.

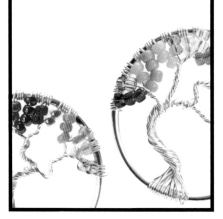

Celtic Colors

Mix and match colored wire for spectacular summer jewelry in a Celtic style with these deceptively simple pieces by Hilary Sahota.

FOR THE BRACELET YOU WILL NEED

1 x 39⅜in (1m) length of US 20-gauge (SWG 21, 0.8mm) wire, turquoise

1 x 39⅜in (1m) length of US 20-gauge (SWG 21, 0.8mm) wire, peridot green

Round-nose pliers

Snipe-nose pliers

Side cutters

Looping pliers or bail-making pliers (optional)

Bracelet

1 For the figure-of-eight make a small loop at one end of your wire. Push the pliers up against the loop and make a large loop at the other end (see page 15). Cut off the excess wire flush against the loop.

2 Repeat this step seven more times with the turquoise wire and the same again in the pale green wire, or until there are enough links for the bracelet. Make sure all of the completed links are the same size.

3 Arrange the links in stacks of two, with alternating colors on the top. You can choose whether to reverse the orientation of the loops as you go.

4 Make your own jumprings by winding wire around a mandrel, pliers, or a knitting needle with a diameter of ³⁄₁₆in (5mm) to make a coil. Use one or both colors of wire, or even a third color if you like. Take a pair of side cutters and snip complete circles of wire off the end of the coil to make matching jumprings.

5 Attach a jumpring to a large loop on one link and a small loop on another link. Stack the two links on top of each other and attach another jumpring to the loops on the other side.

6 Add the next two Celtic links to this jumpring and continue adding jumprings and links until you have your desired length. To finish the bracelet, add an extra pair of jumprings at one end and make a large looped hook at the other.

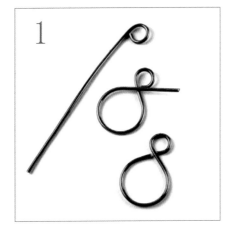

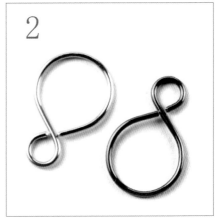

Using looping pliers or bail-making pliers ensures that your loops are exactly the same size every time.

Necklace

YOU WILL NEED

24 x 2in (50mm) lengths of US 20-gauge (SWG 21, 0.8mm) wire, silver-colored

13 x 6mm round pearls

13 x 2in (50mm) eyepins, silver-colored

3 x 6mm jumprings

1 x hook-style clasp

Silver wire Celtic links interspaced with pearls make a lovely summer wedding necklace for a bride or bridesmaid. Just increase the number of links and add pearls with a double loop in between.

Earrings

YOU WILL NEED

2 x 2in (50mm) lengths of US 20-gauge (SWG 21, 0.8mm) wire, turquoise-colored

2 x 2in (50mm) lengths of US 20-gauge (SWG 21, 0.8mm) wire, peridot-colored

2 x 6mm oval beads, peridot

6 x 5mm jumprings, color matched

2 x earwires, color matched

A simple pair of earrings can be made with the Celtic link and a matching bead drop attached to shepherd's hook earwires.

Experiment with different color combinations and loop sizes for unusual designs.

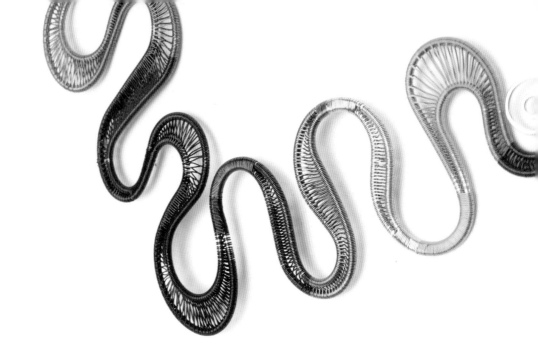

Rainbow
Serpent

This sinuous design by James Ferris for a rainbow serpent will make you a master at weaving. Adapt this concept to any shape, and remember—practice makes perfect!

FOR THE NECKLACE
YOU WILL NEED

1 x reel of US 16-gauge (SWG 18, 1.25mm) wire, silver-plated

1 x reel of US 28-gauge (SWG 30, 0.3mm) wire, various colors

Masking tape

Marker pen

Round multi-mandrel or ring mandrel

Wire wool

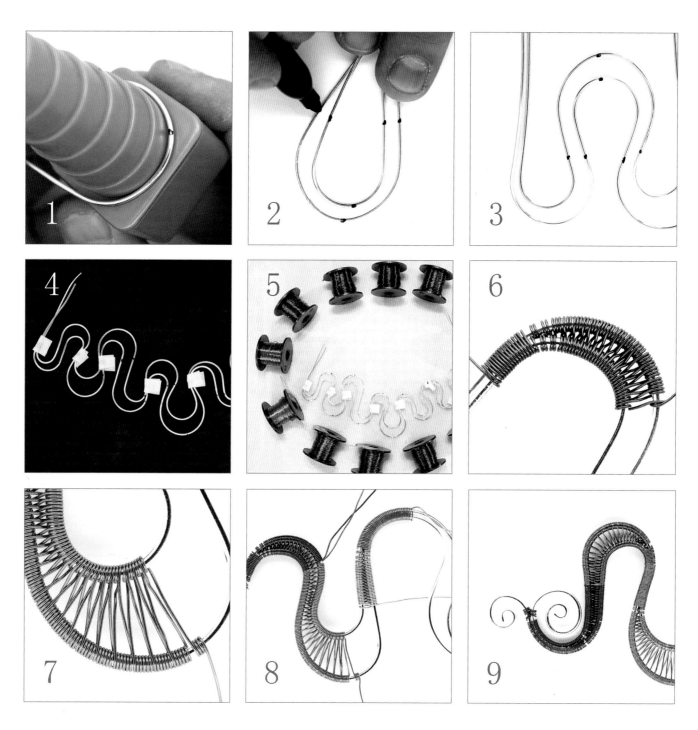

Use copper wire and patinate with liver of sulfur for a different look.

Necklace

1 Cut two lengths of 16-gauge wire at 30in (750mm). Mark the middle of both wires with a marker pen. Starting from the middle of one wire, bend round the largest setting on a round multi-mandrel or a ring mandrel to create a teardrop shape. Do the same with the other wire on the mandrel, but five sizes smaller.

2 Lay the two wires down so the small teardrop is on the inside of the larger one. Using a marker pen, mark both wires roughly where the next bends will start, making the next teardrop shape either side of the first.

3 Starting with what will be the outside wire, make the next two bends a size or two smaller than the center shape, then make the two inside bends. You may find it easier to start with the outside bends so you can judge what kind of gap and shape you are going to weave. Again, make marks where the next bend will go.

4 Continue until you are happy with your design, being careful about the points where the two wires meet. Make the design about 8in (200mm) long overall. It can be any shape, so be creative. When finished, tack the two wires together where they meet by tightly wrapping five times around using some wrapping wire. Stick a small piece of masking tape over the wraps to stop them sliding.

5 Using wire wool, gently rub off the marks made for each of the bends. Place more marks along the design to determine where each shade of wire will begin and end. Lining up the wire in order of color and number helps to prevent confusion.

6 Start wrapping and weaving from one end of the design. Try using 28-gauge wire and leave a tail about 8in (200mm) long, which will be used at the finish. Make your own judgment about how much wire you need; depending on how many colors you use it could be anywhere between 39⅜in (1m) and 98in (2.5m). (See page 18 for a two-wire weave.)

7 As you start to weave around the corners, you will need to add more wraps to the outside bend before you cross over. The wider the gap and tighter the angle the more wraps you will need. This is because there is more wire on the outside bends to cover. Stop weaving when you reach the position shown in the example.

8 Begin wrapping and weaving from the opposite direction. It is easier to weave when the core wires are a constant width or when the core wires are increasing in width. Where the weaves meet, force the last couple of wraps inward to tighten everything up and trim to the outside. This mammoth wrapping and weaving session may take more than ten hours.

9 Finish off the ends by trimming the two inside end wires to 2in (50mm) and spiralling inward toward the design. Trim the outer two wires to 1in (25mm) and spiral toward the outside. With the remaining wrapping wire, weave a few times around to finish off. The outside spirals are for attaching a ribbon, cord, or chain.

Earrings

YOU WILL NEED

4 x 6in (150mm) lengths of US 18-gauge (SWG 19, 1mm) wire, silver-colored

6 x 39⅜in (1m) lengths of US 28-gauge (SWG 30, 0.3mm) wire in various (rainbow) shades

2 x earwires, silver-colored

Use four 6in (150mm) lengths of 16-gauge or 18-gauge wire and make two "S"-shaped frames, but place an eyeloop at the top instead of a spiral.

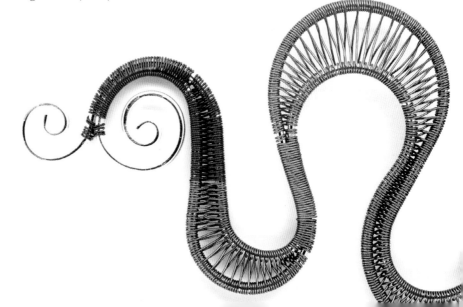

In the Pink

Be pretty in pink with these gorgeous rose-colored pieces, wired with sparkly crystals, by Sian Hamilton.

FOR THE NECKLACE YOU WILL NEED

1 x reel of US 20-gauge (SWG 21, 0.8mm) wire, silver-colored

1 x reel of US 24-gauge (SWG 25, 0.5mm) wire, pink

150 x 4mm rondelle crystals, fuchsia

1 x fine curb chain, silver-colored

3 x 5mm jumprings, silver-colored

1 x clasp with ring, silver-colored

Round-nose pliers

Chain-nose pliers

Side cutters

Necklace

1 Make a template for the petal shape from a piece of spare wire. Bend a section of wire in half, then twist the wire together about 2in (50mm) down from the bend. If the wire has come off a roll it will have a natural bend to make a thin petal shape.

2 Take a 39⅜in (1m) length of 20-gauge silver wire and starting at one end, bend almost in half, about 8in (200mm) in from the end. Shape into a long thin petal, using the template as a guide. Twist twice to secure.

3 Working on the side of the first petal with the longest wire, bend the wire up against the first petal and make another exactly the same size. Twist twice to secure, make three more in the same way. You should have five petals in total.

4 Pull the petals apart and twist them until they are in a flower shape. Bend the two wire ends to a right angle, facing away from the flower.

5 Wrap both wire ends around the center of the flower. This can be as messy as you want. Use all the free wire and finish both ends on the same side, which will be the back.

6 Hook two fingers into each petal and pull the sides out to create a fatter petal shape. All five petals should nearly touch.

7 Take a 20in (500mm) length of colored 24-gauge wire and wrap it onto one of the petals. Start at the base of the petal. Add a crystal and wrap to the opposite side of the petal. Continue adding crystals and wrapping around the sides of the petal.

8 Wrap all five petals in the same way. Make sure you tuck in any wire ends using a pair of chain-nose pliers. Add new sections of wire by wrapping it around the petal edge before adding crystals and carrying on.

9 Decide which petal will be at the top and attach two jumprings. Cut two equal lengths of chain. Attach each length to one of the jumprings and the final ring to the end of one chain. Add a clasp to the other side.

Pendant

YOU WILL NEED

1 x 9½in (240mm) length of US 20-gauge (SWG 21, 0.8mm) wire, copper

1 x 78in (2m) length of US 24-gauge (SWG 25, 0.5mm) wire, bright pink

50 x 4mm crystal beads, bright pink

1 x ready-made chain necklace, copper

Wire-forming jig

The wire technique shown in the main project can be used to create many different shapes. This piece was created with the help of a wire-forming jig, a flat piece of metal or plastic with holes. Pegs are placed in the holes to make a pattern which the wire is formed around.

Earrings

YOU WILL NEED

2 x 6in (150mm) lengths of US 20-gauge (SWG 21, 0.8mm) wire, silver-colored

1 x 39in (1m) lengths of US 24-gauge (SWG 25, 0.5mm) wire, bright pink

50 x 4mm crystal beads, bright pink

2 x earwires, silver-colored

Make two petal shapes with a loop at the top. Cut a piece of 20-gauge wire about 6in (150mm) long and make a loop at one end. About 2in (50mm) along the wire, bend in half then coil the wire just under the loop. Make a petal shape and wrap it with crystals. Attach an earwire to finish.

Color Splash

Sometimes less is more. Add a little splash of color with these simple yet elegant designs by Sue Mason-Burns.

FOR THE RED EARRINGS YOU WILL NEED

1 x reel of US 18-gauge (SWG 19, 1mm) wire, gunmetal

1 x reel of US 28-gauge (SWG 30, 0.3mm) wire, gunmetal

2 x 8mm red crackle glass beads

Side cutters

Small and large bail-making pliers

Ring mandrel

Flat-nose pliers

Round-nose pliers

Chain-nose pliers

Hammer

Steel bench block

Low-tack masking tape

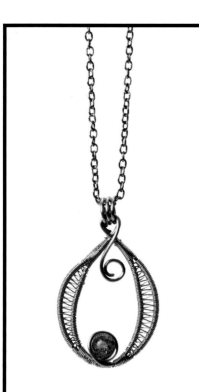

Pendant

YOU WILL NEED

1 x 18in (460mm) lengths of US 19-gauge (SWG 20, 0.9mm) wire, gunmetal-colored

1 x 39⅜in (1m) length of US 28-gauge (SWG 30, 0.3mm) wire, gunmetal-colored

1 x 8mm crackle glass bead, red

1 x ready-made chain, gunmetal-colored

Use the techniques for the earrings to make a pendant to match, with woven sections on both sides and a single bead in the middle. Hang it from a trace chain in matching gunmetal.

Earrings

1   Flush cut 15¾in (400mm) of 18-gauge wire. Turn a loop in one end with the larger jaw of small bail-making pliers (see page 15). Bend the wire around the largest point of a ring mandrel. Position the pliers so the first loop is on the mandrel. Take the wire around the mandrel again to form two identical loops at the top of the hoop.

2   Hold the two loops in place with a ⅛in (3mm) mandrel. Take the tail wire in an arc within the hoop shape, forming a crescent with the outer frame. Bring this wire parallel with the lowest part of the hoop. Secure the frame and the inner wire with a small piece of low-tack masking tape to hold it in place while you weave.

3   Using a 39⅜in (1m) length of 28-gauge wire begin to weave the inside wire of the frame as follows: Coil three times around the wire, pass the wire over this wire and behind the outer wire, and coil this wire four times. Repeat this weave until you reach the tape. Remove the tape and coil ten times around both frame wires. Form a loop in the inner frame wire.

4   Coil the weaving wire ten times around the outer frame, then coil it ten times around both frame wires together, and 15 times around the outer frame. Thread a bead onto the weaving wire and coil five times around the outer frame wire. Form a further loop with the inner frame, framing the bead. Coil the weaving wire around both frame wires 10 times, and form a smaller loop in the inner frame wire.

5   Trim the remaining inner frame wire to a length of approx. 2½in (60mm). Using round-nose pliers, form a decorative inward sweeping spiral to finish the wire. This completes one earring. Repeat the steps to form the other earring, remembering to make the second a mirror image of the first.

6   Cut two 3¼in (80mm) lengths of 18-gauge wire. Use the smaller jaw of small bail-making pliers to make a loop in one end. Bend the wire above this loop around the larger jaw of large bail-making pliers. Trim and bend the tips of the earwires with flat-nose pliers. Hammer the arc of the earwires flat with the hammer. Open the loop and attach loops of earrings to earwires.

You can use mandrels to form the loops within the design, but the wire will naturally loop if you bend it gently.

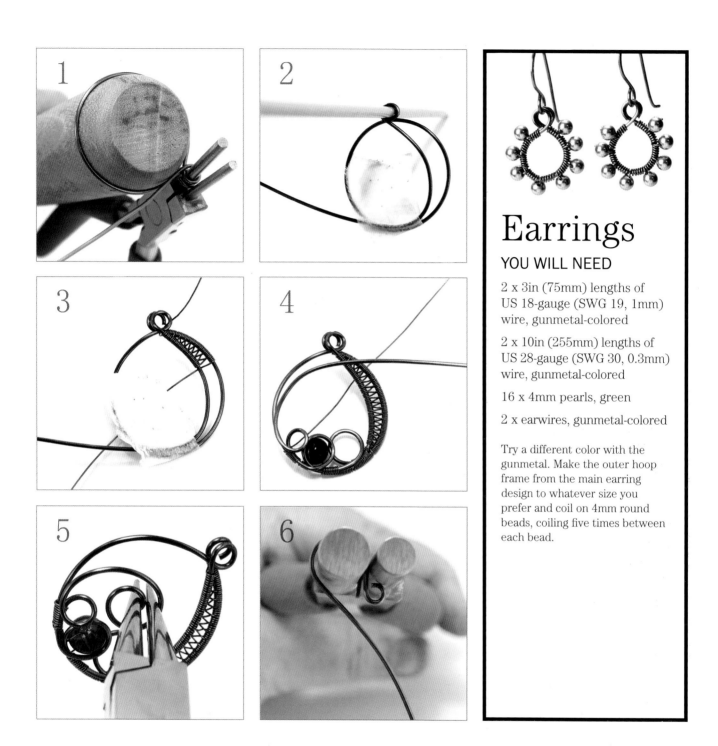

Earrings

YOU WILL NEED

2 x 3in (75mm) lengths of US 18-gauge (SWG 19, 1mm) wire, gunmetal-colored

2 x 10in (255mm) lengths of US 28-gauge (SWG 30, 0.3mm) wire, gunmetal-colored

16 x 4mm pearls, green

2 x earwires, gunmetal-colored

Try a different color with the gunmetal. Make the outer hoop frame from the main earring design to whatever size you prefer and coil on 4mm round beads, coiling five times between each bead.

To prevent the earwires from bending out of shape when worn, use the nylon side of the hammer to harden them.

Tapestry Weave

Create this intricately woven set designed by Sue Mason-Burns, with a tapestry-effect pattern that uses complementary colored wires as "thread".

FOR THE BRACELET YOU WILL NEED

1 x reel of US 18-gauge (SWG 19, 1mm) wire, gunmetal

1 x reel of US 28-gauge (SWG 30, 0.3mm) wire, dark purple and vivid green

Side cutters

Flat-nose pliers

Round-nose pliers

Chain-nose pliers

Clear nail varnish

Small and large bail-making pliers

Hammer

Steel bench block

Oval bracelet mandrel

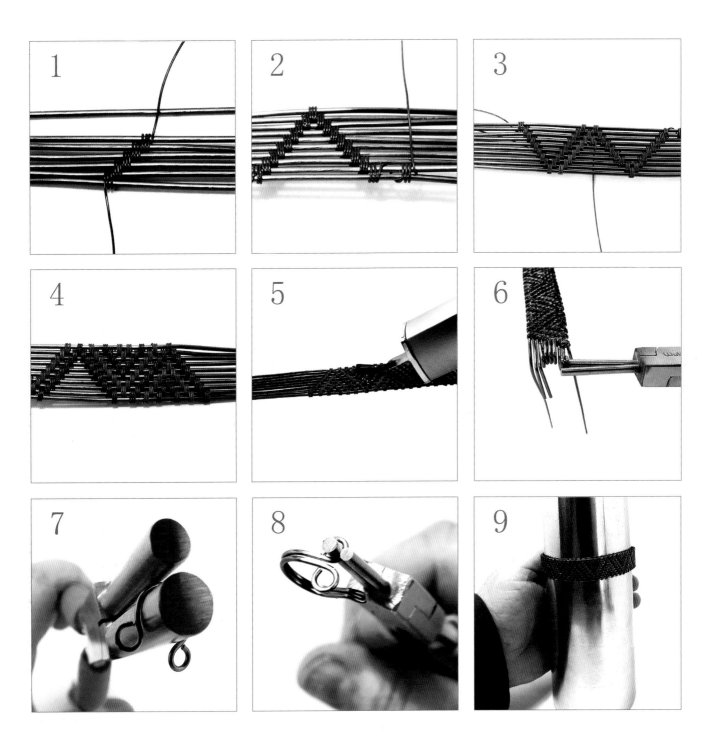

Snip the end off the weaving wire regularly to help you feed it between the frame wires. If you are having trouble threading the wire through the frame wires, try using fine-tipped tweezers to part them.

Bracelet

1 Flush cut and straighten ten 11¾in (300mm) lengths of 18-gauge gunmetal wire and a 79in (2m) length of purple 28-gauge wire (see page 20). Leave a 4in (100mm) tail and beginning 2in (50mm) from the end of the wire, coil the weaving wire three times around two parallel lengths of 18-gauge wire. Take the wire between these two wires. Add another 18-gauge wire and coil three times around the upper original wire and the new wire.

2 Take the wire between the two upper wires and continue adding wires in this way until you have a diagonal line of weaving working its way up the frame wires. Work your way down the other side of the triangle, weaving the same pairs of wires to mirror the upward diagonal line of the triangle. Leave a space equal to the apex of the triangle and weave seven further triangles.

3 Turn the frame 180 degrees. Weave a line of triangles in the green wire, beginning inside the first upward diagonal of the purple triangles, so they will fit between the first line of woven triangles. Repeat the steps for the line of purple triangles and complete the row of green triangles, with the apex of each sitting on the second frame wire in from the edge of the bracelet frame.

4 Cut a length of purple wire about 20in (500mm) long. Leaving a 2in (50mm) tail, begin inside the first green triangle. Complete the weave as in Step 1 to form an inner triangle. Weave so there is one full frame wire between the upper wire of the apex of the inner triangle and the lower wire of the outer triangle. Trim and secure the tail wires.

5 Repeat this process until you have a line of inner triangles in opposite colorways within each triangle. When all the triangles are complete, turn to the back of the work. Make sure all trimmed tail wires are flush with the frame and paint clear nail varnish across all the weaving wires. This will stop the weave unravelling and prevent the wire from scratching the wearer. Leave to dry.

6 Using flat-nose pliers, bend the middle four frame wires up toward the back of the bracelet to a 90-degree angle. Bend the four wires again ⅛in (2mm) along the length, so that they are parallel to the bracelet frame. Trim to ⅜in (10mm) and bend the tips down at a 90-degree angle. Bend the next two wires to 90 degrees in the opposite direction and trim to ⅜in (10mm) and form loops (see page 15).

7 Form the remaining two wires into decorative spirals to sit against the front of the bracelet. Make the eye part of the clasp component by forming loops in each end of 2½in (60mm) of 18-gauge wire. Center on the larger jaw of large bail-making pliers and bring the two loops together. Hammer the rounded part of the eye flat with the metal side of the hammer on the steel bench block.

8 Cut a 3¼in (80mm) length of 18-gauge wire for the hook. Fold in half around the tip of round-nose pliers. Use flat-nose pliers to bring the two wires together parallel. Bend the folded end slightly. Bend the parallel wires around the large bail-making pliers and make loops using small bail-making pliers. Open the loops made at Step 7 and attach each of these components.

9 Form the shape of the bracelet around an oval bracelet mandrel, pressing the bracelet against the mandrel firmly to help retain the shape. When the two components of the clasp come together, remove the bracelet from the mandrel, close the clasp, and continue to manipulate the bracelet with your fingers until you are happy with the shape

Pendant

YOU WILL NEED

20 x 4in (100mm) lengths of US 18-gauge (SWG 19, 1mm) wire, gunmetal-colored

1 x 78in (2m) length of US 28-gauge (SWG 30, 0.3mm) wire, vivid green

1 x 78in (2m) length of US 28-gauge (SWG 30, 0.3mm) wire, dark purple

1 x chain to match

Use the techniques for making the triangle to create a diamond shape with 20 x 4in (100mm) lengths of 18-gauge frame wire. Form decorative spirals in the ends of these wires. Form both the ends of the uppermost frame wire into a loop and hang the finished pendant from a chain threaded through a jumpring attached to this loop.

Emerald Chandelier

Be bold with this opulent collection by Sue Mason-Burns. Dramatic chandeliers formed from a wire framework make a perfect base from which to dangle some bling!

FOR THE EARRINGS YOU WILL NEED

1 x reel of US 20-gauge (SWG 21, 0.8mm) wire, light gold

1 x reel of US 28-gauge (SWG 30, 0.3mm) wire, light gold

2 x 24mm oval faceted crystals, blue-green

6 x 8mm twist faceted crystals, blue-green

Side cutters

Flat-nose pliers

Round-nose pliers

Chain-nose pliers

Medium and large bail-making pliers

Hammer

Steel bench block

Earrings

1 Cut 6in (150mm) of 18-gauge wire and form a wrapped loop in one end (see page 16). Thread on an oval crystal and finish with a wrapped loop. Trim the tail wires with a flush cutter, making sure they are both on the same side of the loops, which will be at the back of your design.

2 Flush-cut three lengths of 18-gauge wire, approx. 18in (450mm) long, and a 39⅜in (1m) length of 28-gauge wire. Holding the three wires together parallel and leaving a short tail with the 28-gauge wire, begin weaving 11¾in (300mm) from one end. Coil three times around the bottom wire, three times around the bottom and middle wires together, three times around all three wires, and three times around the two lower wires again. Repeat five times.

3 Gently curve the woven section to match the curve of the crystal. Wrap the longer tails of wire 360 degrees around the upper wrapped loop, and the remaining three tails 180 degrees around the lower loop. Trim the 28-gauge wire tails.

4 Take the bottom and middle of the three upper tail wires that were just wrapped around the upper loop in an arc along the face of the crystal. Wrap them once around the lower loop.

5 Flush cut the remaining tail wire to approx. 1¾in (30mm) and, using round-nose pliers, form into a decorative open spiral. This should sit over the two wires running along the crystal and in the space between the woven section and these two wires.

6 Wrap the three lower tail wires around the lower loops once more and trim with side cutters. Use flat-nose pliers to gently press these trimmed wires into the back of your work so that they remain secure.

7 Flush cut the remaining two lower tail wires to ¾in (20mm). Using the smaller jaw of medium bail-making pliers, form a loop in an inward direction with each of these tail wires. These will form the two upper chandelier loops from which to hang your decorative crystals.

8 Cut three 3¼in (80mm) lengths of 18-gauge wire. Form a small coil in one end of each length, to act as a decorative headpin. Thread an 8mm crystal onto each headpin and turn a simple loop. Open the loops in the tops of each of the headpins and attach the crystals to the lower loops of the earring design. Make a second earring as a mirror image.

9 Cut two 4in (100mm) lengths of 18-gauge wire and turn a loop at one end of each. Using the larger jaw of large bail-making pliers, bend the hook part of the earwires. Trim and turn the ends up with flat-nose pliers. Hammer the bends of the earwires flat. Open the loops and attach to the upper loop of the earrings.

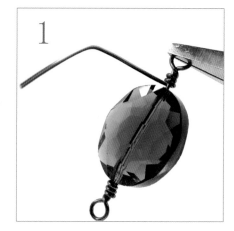

Ensure both earwires are identical by making them at the same time.

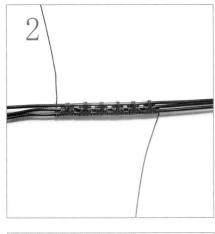

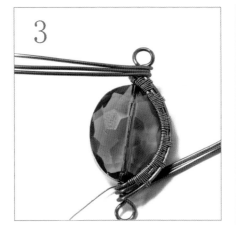

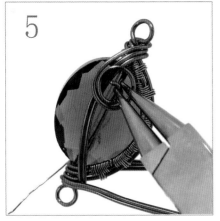

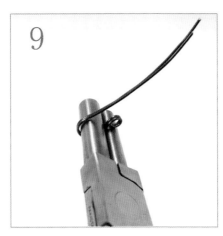

Before you cover any part of a bead with wire wrapping, be sure to wipe any finger marks off the bead.

Pendant

YOU WILL NEED

1 x 60in (1.5m) length of US 18-gauge (SWG 19, 1mm) wire, light gold-colored

1 x 78in (2m) length of US 28-gauge (SWG 30, 0.3mm) wire, light gold-colored

3 x 5mm jumprings, light gold-colored

1 x 24mm oval faceted crystal, blue-green

3 x 10mm briolette crystals, blue-green

1 x ready-made chain, light gold-colored

Follow the same pattern as for the earrings, but instead of the simple crisscross at the lower loop, add some decorative loops and a simple figure-of-eight woven section to the front of your pendant.

Fall Filigree

Use filigree links and vibrant-colored beads to make this statement set by Jayne Rimington. With this versatile design you can create something truly unique.

FOR THE NECKLACE YOU WILL NEED

1 x 5ft (1.6m) length of US 20-gauge (SWG 21, 0.8mm) wire

1 x 4ft (1.3m) length of US 26-gauge (SWG 27, 0.4mm) wire

23 x semiprecious beads, jade

46 x beadcaps or spacer beads

90 x 5mm red-colored jumprings

1 x 8in (200mm) chain

1 x toggle clasp

1 x headpin

Round-nose pliers

Chain-nose pliers

Dowel (optional)

Side cutters

Bracelet

YOU WILL NEED

3 x 6in (150mm) lengths of US 20-gauge (SWG 21, 0.8mm) wire, silver-colored (for filigree shapes)

4 x 4in (100mm) lengths of US 20-gauge (SWG 21, 0.8mm) wire, silver-colored (for wrapped eyepins)

6 x 1in (25mm) lengths of US 26-gauge (SWG 27, 0.4mm) wire, silver-colored

2 x 2in (50mm) headpins, silver-colored

4 x 8mm jade beads, red

12 x 5mm jumprings, red

8 x 4mm daisy spacers, silver-colored

1 x toggle clasp, silver-colored

Use the same method to construct the wire links and bead elements. Link together to the required length, adding a chain if required, and add a toggle clasp.

Necklace

1   Using pliers or dowel, form a figure-of-eight with the 20-gauge wire. Work from bottom to top so the ends of the wire will be opposite each other, and easier to finish off. Each link uses approx. 6in (150mm) of wire.

2   Remove the pliers or dowel from the last loop and place alongside. Form another figure-of-eight on top, keeping the wire taut so the loops are the same size. When four loops have been made, cut the wire.

3   Secure the link shape in the middle using the 26-gauge wire to wrap near the center. Keep the wire taut and wrap at least three times each side of the center. Trim the ends of wires using cutters and pliers.

4   Using round-nose pliers, curl the ends of the 20-gauge wire inward. If you loop the ends in opposite directions both will be visible and decorative. Repeat Steps 1–4 to create the links required; for this necklace you will need ten links.

5   Lay out the finished links and plan the design. Select beads and place between links to see how the necklace will look. Choose spacers, beadcaps, and jumprings.

6   Using a wire-wrapped bead with daisy spacers, make up the bead elements between the links. Make a wrapped loop (see page 16) on the end using the 20-gauge wire and thread on a daisy spacer, a jade bead, and a daisy spacer. Make a wrapped loop at the end and cut off the excess wire. Make 22 in total. Add two red jumprings to each end of the bead elements.

7   Link the chain and bead elements. Lay out each row as it is completed to help you to visualize the finished piece. For the central pendant bead use a headpin, make a wrapped loop and attach it to the link (see page 16). Plan the vertical and diagonal connecting pieces.

8   Lay out the linked design and measure the required length of the chain. You may need to adjust the chain length or add bead elements near the top of the design to make it sit correctly.

9   Finish by making a clasp. A toggle clasp has been used for the example because it is easy to use and helps with the drape of this intricate design.

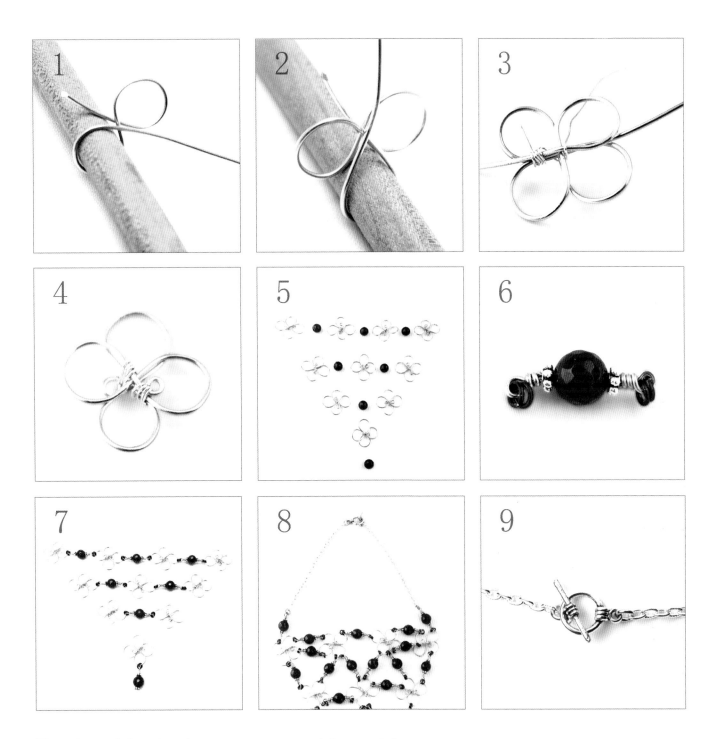

To give this design extra sparkle, add
a crystal to the center of the filigree link.

Amethyst Moon

Showcase nature's bounty by framing a stunning natural amethyst cabochon with vintage bronze wire in this exquisite collection by Sue Mason-Burns.

FOR THE NECKLACE YOU WILL NEED

1 x reel of US 20-gauge (SWG 21, 0.8mm) square wire, vintage bronze

1 x reel of US 18-gauge (SWG 19, 1mm) half-round wire, vintage bronze

1 x reel of US 18-gauge (SWG 19, 1mm) round wire, vintage bronze

1 x 30mm diameter round amethyst with bronze cabochon

6 x 10mm chevron amethyst round beads

6 x 8mm faceted chevron amethyst beads

Side cutters

Flat-nose pliers

Wire-twisting pliers

¼in (7mm) round mandrel

Round-nose pliers

Chain-nose pliers

Medium and large bail-making pliers

Marker pen

Ruler

Low-tack masking tape

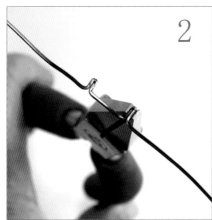

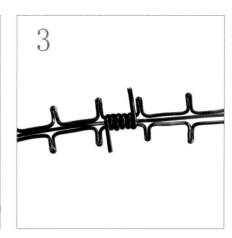

Necklace

1 Cut two 11¾in (300mm) lengths and one 8in (200mm) length of square wire. Mark the center point of each of the 11¾in (300mm) wires. Hold this point with the tip of flat-nose pliers and bend the wire in half. Squeeze together at the fold and hold with the flat-nose pliers. Bend each side up so the wire runs horizontally.

2 Mark points ⅜in (10mm) on either side of the first prong. Hold the wire on this mark with the flat-nose pliers and bend up 90 degrees for the next prong. Continue as in Step 1 until there are ten prongs on each wire.

3 Lay the wires parallel so the prongs meet, and lay the 8in (200mm) wire between them. Tape the ends of the wires to hold them together. Cut 2½in (60mm) of half-round wire. Wrap the half-round wire around the three parallel wires between the prongs, working from the center out. Repeat between each of the prongs.

4 Remove the tape. Working from the center out using flat-nose pliers, bend the wrapped wires gently around the cabochon. Flatten the prongs against the front and back as you go. Where the wires meet at the top, bend each up to a 90-degree angle. Secure by coiling twice with one of these wires.

5 Grip the end of this wire with wire-twisting pliers and twist until you are happy with the effect. Trim the end of the wire—which has been marked by the twisting pliers—and form a closed spiral (see page 17) to sit at the front of the cabochon. Repeat for the tail wire on the opposite side.

6 Take the two central wires and form a bail around a ¼in (7mm) mandrel, such as a knitting needle. Coil twice around the base of the bail with a tail wire, leaving the three tail wires to the rear of the cabochon. Trim these to around ⅝in (15mm) and finish with a small loop. Twist and spiral the final wire above the two spirals as in Step 5.

7 Cut 6in (150mm) of 18-gauge wire. Form a loop with the smaller jaw of medium bail-making pliers. Thread on a 10mm bead and form a loop at the other end. Spiral the tail wire along the length of the bead, finishing at the opposite loop. Trim and secure. Cut 2½in (60mm) of 18-gauge wire. Form a loop, thread on an 8mm bead, and form a loop in the opposite direction.

8 Make chain links by forming a loop at the end of the 18-gauge wire, still on the spool, around the smaller jaw of medium bail-making pliers. Reposition this jaw to the point where the first loop begins. Form a loop in the opposite direction until the wires cross, and flush cut. Make a further link for the eye of the clasp using the larger jaw of the pliers.

9 For the hook, bend a 2½in (60mm) length of wire in half using round-nose pliers. Using flat-nose pliers, gently squeeze the two halves of the wire together and bend the folded end of the wire lightly. Bend it around the larger jaw of large bail-making pliers. Form outward loops in each of the tail wires with the smaller jaw of medium bail-making pliers.

To protect the cabochon, use flat-nose pliers coated with a rubber-coating solution.

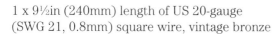

Earrings

YOU WILL NEED

2 x 15mm round amethysts with bronze cabochon

1 x 9½in (240mm) length of US 20-gauge (SWG 21, 0.8mm) square wire, vintage bronze

1 x 6in (150mm) length of US 18-gauge (SWG 19, 1mm) half-round wire, vintage bronze

2 x 6mm round beads, amethyst

2 x earwires, vintage bronze

Use the same techniques as your cabochon focal to frame some smaller amethyst cabochons, leaving out the central wire. Hang from handmade earwires, decorated with a 6mm amethyst round bead.

Ring

YOU WILL NEED

2 x 20in (510mm) lengths of US 18-gauge (SWG 19, 1mm) round wire, vintage bronze

1 x 25mm rectangle amethyst cabochon

Wrap two 20in (500mm) lengths of 18-gauge round wire around a ring mandrel to form the shank. Use the remaining tails to secure a matching rectangular amethyst cabochon, finishing with decorative open spirals.

Crystal Dewdrops

Inspired by delicate drops of dew on leaves, these pretty pieces by Lisa Floyd combine versatility with style for a wire flower and crystal brooch that can be added to a simple necklace, and a statement ring.

FOR THE BROOCH/NECKLACE YOU WILL NEED

1 x reel of US 20-gauge (SWG 21, 0.8mm) wire

1 x reel of US 22-gauge (SWG 23, 0.6mm) wire

1 x reel of US 26-gauge (SWG 27, 0.4mm) wire

1 x 13/16in (20mm) sieve and brooch back

5 x 6mm bicone crystals, clear

16 x 4mm bicone crystals, black diamond

4 x crystals (optional)

1 x 14in (350mm) length of 0.8mm round beaded thread, semiprecious cherry glass beads

4 x 4mm metal round beads, beadcaps, and crimps

2 x wire guards

2 x 9mm jumprings, soldered

Round-nose pliers

Flat-nose pliers

Chain-nose pliers

Clear monofilament

Clear nail varnish to seal knot

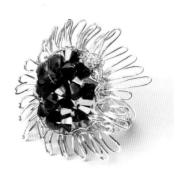

Working from longer, continuous lengths of wire will help give the wirework more strength and rigidity.

Brooch

1. Working from the reel if possible, make the main flower shape. Allow a generous length of 20-gauge wire then, working from its center, begin to form long, narrow petal shapes. Use your fingers to form the loops, helping the process with round-nose pliers if necessary. Avoid gripping the wire with the pliers and marking it.

2. Keeping the petals close in size and shape, continue until you have enough for the basis of a flower. Using the same technique, make a second row that is smaller in size and doubles back to run alongside the first. Take your time to ensure that the petals are regular and sit neatly. Spread out the petals at the top, keeping the bottom loops tighter together.

3. Use 22-gauge wire to secure the petals. Again working from a reel, allow a generous length of wire and, working from its center, join the petal end sections. Working in one direction, take one length and continue placing it over and under the base loops of the two rows of petals to secure them. Leave spare wire at this stage for further working.

4. Using the techniques shown in Steps 1–3, create a third row of petals even smaller in size. Secure to the other petals using the 22-gauge wire in the same over-and-under formation, alternating its placement to the first row. Aim for a regular pattern, ensuring that all petals are secure and leaving spare wire. Use flat-nose pliers to help to gently bend the petal tops into a natural, curved effect. Ideally, all spare wire should be worked so it ends at the same section.

5. Using the remaining 20-gauge wire, create two simple leaf shapes from one piece. Wrap leaf bases with the 22-gauge wire to secure.

6. Use 22-gauge wire to secure the clear crystals; the example uses five in total. Working from a reel, allow a length of wire, and working from its center, start coiling around one of the leaves. Add 6mm clear crystal bicone beads, continuing to coil the wire to keep each one in place and sitting at the same angle. Wire wrap at the base of the leaves for added strength.

7. Use 26-gauge wire for the 4mm bicone crystals to complete the center area of the flower. Work in one direction adding two beads before threading and returning the wire through the loops at the base of the petals. Add more beads in this pattern to complete a circle before working inward to cover the space. The excess wire can be placed under and over the petals again to add detail and strength.

8. Use 26-gauge wire to attach the sieve to the rear of the flower. Check positioning on your neck, adjust the angle to suit and slot on the back section. Secure using chain-nose pliers. If you want to prevent the brooch part from showing through the crystal center, add a few 4mm crystals to the middle of the sieve using clear monofilament before attaching. Knot and secure.

9. To transform the brooch into a choker-style necklace that is simply hooked together, place semiprecious beads on a thread approx. 14in (350mm) long, adjusting as required. Add a 4mm metal bead, crimp, beadcap, round bead, beadcap, crimp, and metal bead. Add a wire guard and a large soldered jumpring. Return the thread through all findings and secure the crimps. Tighten and repeat for the other side.

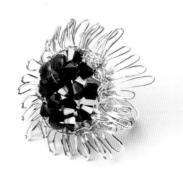

Ring

YOU WILL NEED

1 x reel of US 22-gauge (SWG 23, 0.6mm) wire

1 x reel of US 26-gauge (SWG 27, 0.4mm) wire

16 x 4mm bicone crystals, jet

Make a ring in the same way as the brooch but using a smaller gauged wire for a delicate finish. Wire-wrap the ring shape using a mandrel or suitably sized dowel.

Don't abandon first attempts that have uneven petal sizes, as they can still look effective.

Egyptian Torque

Walk like an Egyptian with this classic torque necklace and upper-arm bracelet by Sue Mason-Burns. Crafted in copper, the simplicity of the single wire contrasts with the intricate weaving that is at the heart of these striking pieces.

FOR THE NECKLACE YOU WILL NEED

1 x reel of US 10-gauge (SWG 12, 2.5mm) wire, copper

1 x reel of US 18-gauge (SWG 19, 1mm) wire, copper

1 x reel of US 26-gauge (SWG 27, 0.4mm) wire, copper

1 x 18mm x 13mm teardrop, faceted crystal bead, green millefiori

Low-tack masking tape

Pencil and paper

Liver of sulfur

Rubber gloves

Safety goggles

Side cutters

Round-nose pliers

Necklace mandrel

Hammer (one metal and one nylon head)

Steel bench block

Files and emery boards

4mm round mandrel

Large bail-making pliers

Chain-nose pliers

Necklace

1 Flush cut four 15¾in (400mm) lengths of 18-gauge wire. Line up so they are parallel and tape together. Find and mark the center point. Trace around the shape of the bead with a pencil and paper. Using this tracing, measure from the lower center to the top of the bead. Mark this measurement on the taped wires from the center point on both sides.

2 Take 39⅜in (1m) of 26-gauge wire and leave a 11¾in (300mm) tail. Beginning at the center point, coil once around the first wire and once around wires one and two. Bring the wire between these wires and coil once around wires two and three, between these wires and once around wires three and four, then once around wire four.

3 Take the wire behind wires four and three, coil around wire three, behind wires three and two, around wire two, behind wires two and one, and wire one. Weave until you reach the mark made at Step 1. Repeat this process for the opposite side. Thread the bead onto the central tail wires. In the center of the woven section, thread the tail wires with the bead attached through the top woven wire and back up through the bead. Bend each side of the woven wire around the bead. Using each tail wire in turn, weave one turn.

4 Trim and secure the tail wires. Fold the two sets of four wires across the back of the work and trim each to a length of 4¾in (120mm). Use the metal side of the hammer and a steel bench block to hammer the two sets of wires flat. File the ends smooth, using a series of progressively finer files followed by emery boards.

5 Coil the flattened wires around a ³⁄₁₆in (4mm) round mandrel, slightly bigger than the wire used for the torque; a knitting needle is ideal. Continue coiling with each set of wires, on both sides of your central focal, until all the wire is coiled. Make sure the ends of the wires are pressed firmly into the circular shape of the mandrel.

6 Flush cut a 23⅝in (600mm) length of 10-gauge wire and form an open spiral to one end. Wrap the wire around the neck section of the necklace mandrel, so it sits just on the collarbone area. Hammer into shape using the nylon side of the hammer. Thread on the woven bead and finish the torque with a matching spiral. Hammer both spirals so they sit flat.

7 Flush cut 3¼in (80mm) of 18-gauge wire to make the hook of a hook and eye clasp. Turn a loop in one end and form the shape around the larger jaw of large bail-making pliers. Finish with a small loop. Hammer the hook flat with the metal side of the hammer. Attach to one spiral of the necklace using a jumpring.

8 Using the smaller jaw of large bail-making pliers, make the eye of a hook and eye clasp. Form a loop at the end of a 2¾in (70mm) length of 18-gauge wire and an identical loop at the other end, in the opposite direction to the first. Trim any excess and hammer flat. Attach to the remaining spiral of the necklace with a jumpring.

9 Fill a glass or plastic bowl with warm water and add a few drops of liver of sulfur. Fill another bowl with cold water. Dip the finished necklace into the liver of sulfur solution and immediately plunge into the cold water. Repeat the process until the copper achieves the desired level of oxidation.

If you prefer a bright copper effect, coat your copper piece with a wax polish to help prevent the oxidation process.

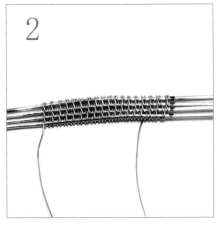

2

3

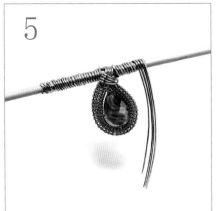

5

6

8

9

Bracelet

YOU WILL NEED

2 x 18mm x 13mm crystal teardrop faceted bead, green millefiori

1 x 22in (560mm) length of US 10-gauge (SWG 12, 2.5mm) wire, copper

4 x 16in (400mm) lengths of US 18-gauge (SWG 19, 1mm) wire, copper

1 x 39⅜in (1m) length of US 26-gauge (SWG 27, 0.4mm) wire, copper

To make a bracelet designed to be worn on the upper arm, use the same technique as for the torque necklace, forming around a bracelet mandrel. Add the woven bead in the same way as before, but with shorter wrapped sections.

If you don't have liver of sulfur, you can oxidize copper by cutting a hard-boiled egg in half and placing it in a sealed container with your piece of jewelry until the desired oxidation is achieved.

Blue Zebra

Play with texture and colour to create these vibrant multi-toned bracelets by Sue Mason-Burns. Eye-catching striped beads are the focus of these safari-inspired bracelets.

FOR THE BANGLE YOU WILL NEED

1 x reel of US 18-gauge (SWG 19, 1mm) wire, black

1 x reel of US 18-gauge (SWG 19, 1mm) square wire, antique copper

1 x reel of US 18-gauge (SWG 19, 1mm) wire, gunmetal

1 x reel of US 20-gauge (SWG 21, 0.8mm) square wire, copper

1 x reel of US 18-gauge (SWG 19, 1mm) half-round wire, antique copper

1 x reel of US 24-gauge (SWG 25, 0.5mm) wire, gunmetal

1 x 30mm zebra coin bead, stabilized turquoise, blue-brown

6 x 6mm zebra, stabilized turquoise beads, blue-brown

Side cutters

Twisting pliers

Flat-nose pliers

Round-nose pliers

Oval bracelet mandrel

Large and small bail-making pliers

Masking tape

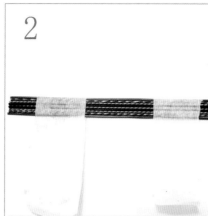
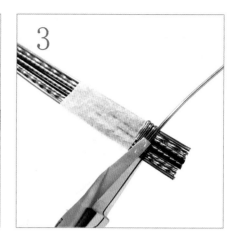

Bangle

1 Flush cut 10in (250mm) lengths
of wire as follows: Two black, two
antique copper, two gunmetal, and
three copper. Use twisting pliers to
twist the square wires. Secure one
end in a vice, grip the other end with
the pliers, and lock in place using the
sliding locking mechanism. Pull the
twisting mechanism at the base of the
pliers, and at the same time release
your grip on the pliers. If you do not
have twisting pliers, use any standard
pliers and twist manually with your
hands, holding the pliers closed.

2 Line up the wires in this order:
Gunmetal, twisted antique copper,
twisted copper, black, twisted copper,
black, twisted copper, twisted antique
copper, gunmetal. Use masking tape
to hold them together at ⅝in (15mm)
and 2⁹⁄₁₆in (65mm) from the end.

3 Flush-cut two 2½in (60mm) lengths
of half-round wire. Use flat-nose
pliers to bend one end back on itself,
making a squared hook shape. Hook
over the wires to be wrapped and
secure with the flat-nose pliers. Wrap
around all wires and secure again
with flat-nose pliers. Continue this
process until you have five wraps.
Trim and secure. Repeat at the other
taped section, making four wraps.

4 Bend the four wires on each side away
from the central twisted copper wire.
Thread the coin bead onto the central
copper wire and run the two black
wires behind the bead. Gently bend
the remaining wires around the shape
of the edges of the coin bead until
they meet on the other side. Tape in
place and wrap with half-round wire
as in Step 3.

5 Measure 2in (50mm) from the
wrapped section in Step 4 and wrap
again, as in Step 3, for the opposite
end of the bracelet. Trim all wires
to ⅜in (10mm) beyond the wrapped
section. Fold the inner five wires
inward, over the wrapped section,
and secure. Leave the two outer
wires on each side to make loops
to attach the clasp.

6 Form the shanks of the bracelet
around an oval bracelet mandrel until
there is a gap of around ¾in (20mm)
between each end of the bracelet to
leave room for the clasp.

7 Flush cut a 2½in (60mm) length of
18-gauge gunmetal wire and turn a
loop at each end. Grip the center of
the wire with the smaller jaw of large
bail-making pliers and wrap the wire
around the larger jaw. Cut an 3¼in
(80mm) length of 18-gauge gunmetal
wire. Fold in half around the tip of
round-nose pliers. Use flat-nose pliers
to bring the two wires parallel and
bend the folded end slightly. Bend the
parallel wires around the large bail-
making pliers and make loops with
the small bail-making pliers.

8 Using round-nose pliers, make
loops for attaching the clasp in the
remaining wires at the ends of the
bracelet. Slip on the loops of the clasp
components and close the loops
of the bracelet.

9 Cut two 8in (200mm) lengths of
24-gauge gunmetal wire and secure
onto the two black wires to the rear
of the focal bead, in the gap between
the bead and the first wrapped
section. Thread on a 6mm bead and
coil around the frame wires. Add two
more beads in this way and finish by
coiling around the black wires again.
Trim and secure. Repeat for the
opposite side.

Twisting pliers will twist square wire, but they will also straighten round wire, making it easier to wrap in designs like this.

Memory-wire bracelet

YOU WILL NEED

3 x coils of memory wire, bracelet length

46 x 4mm bicone crystals, jet black

48 x mixed size zebra beads, stabilized turquoise, blue-brown

To make matching a bracelet, cut a three-coil length of bracelet memory wire and turn a loop in one end. Use memory wire round nose pliers if possible as they make looping far easier, though you can still achieve a loop using standard round-nose pliers. Thread on graduating sizes of blue-brown zebra beads, interspersed with 6mm black bicone crystals. Stop when about ½in (13mm) of wire is left. Turn another loop at the end of the memory wire.

Beautiful Burlesque

Combine dramatic wirework shapes and beautiful beads to create this burlesque-style set by Jayne Rimington. Delicate organza contrasts perfectly with the structured wire.

FOR THE NECKLACE YOU WILL NEED

1 x 8ft (2.4m) length of US 18-gauge (SWG 19, 1mm) wire

1 x 22ft (6.8m) length of US 28-gauge (SWG 30, 0.3mm) wire

6 x 8mm faceted Malay jade beads, green

1 x ½oz (10g) bag 3mm (size 8) seed beads, trans-rainbow emerald green

4 x 5mm jumprings

1 x organza and cord necklace

1 x toggle clasp

Nylon jaw pliers

Bail-making pliers or dowel

Round-nose pliers

Side cutters

Necklace

1 Cut 18-gauge wire into six 6⁵⁄₁₆in (160mm) lengths. Make a small loop at each end of the lengths (see page 15) using round-nose pliers, then bend into an "S"-shape using the nylon jaw pliers.

2 For the three-loop links, cut the 18-gauge wire into two lengths of at least 6⁵⁄₁₆in (160mm). Make a small loop at each end using round-nose pliers. Make the first large loop in the center of the wire using a dowel or bail-making pliers, then make a loop on either side. Bring the ends up to the top of the link.

3 Lay your link shapes out to create your design. You may wish to use more or fewer link shapes than here. Note where the wired anchor points should be placed to hold the links together. It may be useful to sketch this out on a notepad to refer to as you piece together the links.

4 Wire the beads onto the links using the 28-gauge wire. Sit the green jade beads into the three-loop link and wire through the bead holes and around the frame. Attach the seed beads to each end of the "S"-shaped link by wiring into the small loops at the ends.

5 Lay out the links with the beads again and review the design that you require before wiring shapes together. At this point you may wish to make additional links or remove some. You may also wish to add additional beads into the spaces.

6 Wire the links together working from the bottom of the design up. Cut around 8in (200mm) of 28-gauge wire for each anchor point. Ensure the wire is tightly wrapped and when trimmed, use pliers to tuck the ends in. Once the links are secured, attach the necklace. For the example, an organza and cord necklace was used and a toggle clasp with jumprings added. The necklace threads through the top loops of the wired shape.

Earrings

YOU WILL NEED

2 x 6in (150mm) lengths
of US 20-gauge (SWG 21,
0.8mm) wire, black-coated

4 x 4in (100mm) lengths
of US 28-gauge (SWG 30,
0.3mm) wire, black-coated

4 x 2.5mm (size 8) seed beads

4 x 6mm jumprings, black

2 x earwires, silver-colored

Make matching earrings by using
an "S"-shaped wire link and wire
wrapping beads on the link to
give it sparkle. Add jumprings
and attach to wire earhooks.

Bag charm

YOU WILL NEED

1 x 1in (25mm) length of
large-link chain

4 x 6in (150mm) lengths
of US 20-gauge (SWG 21,
0.8mm) wire, black-coated

2 x 4in (100mm) lengths
of US 28-gauge (SWG 30,
0.3mm) wire, black-coated

100 x 2.5mm (size 8) seed
beads, emerald green

8 x 8mm faceted Malay jade
beads, green

14 x 2in (50mm) headpins,
silver-colored

1 x bag charm clasp

Using a bag charm clasp, attach
a 1¾₁₆in (30mm) length of chain
by opening the top link or use a
jumpring. Attach an "S"-shaped
link at the bottom of the chain.
Construct charms by using
headpins and matching beads
used in the necklace and earrings,
and also the three-loop wire links.
Attach the charms onto the chain
by using jumprings.

Various tools can be
used to create wire
loops, but using bail-
making pliers or a
dowel will help you
to make consistently
sized loops.

Using nylon-jaw
pliers will prevent
scratches on wire
and are handy for
removing kinks.

Valentine

Open up your heart to this simple and versatile collection by Sian Hamilton—the perfect set to wear on Valentine's Day.

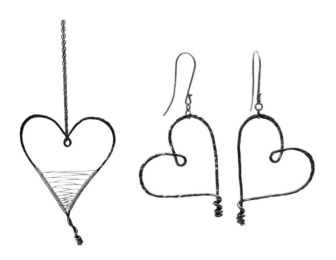

FOR THE NECKLACE YOU WILL NEED

1 x reel of US 16-gauge (SWG 18, 1.25mm) wire, copper

1 x reel of US 24-gauge (SWG 25, 0.5mm) wire, colored

2 x 10mm copper jumprings

1 x large-link chain

1 x clasp

Round-nose pliers

Flat-nose pliers

Side cutters

Hammer

Steel block

Necklace

1 Hold the center of an 11¾in (300mm) length of 16-gauge copper wire in round-nose pliers—it doesn't have to be exact. Fold the wire around the pliers to form a loop so the wires cross. Take the wire in your hands and manipulate it into a heart shape with the wires crossing at the base. Make three hearts—one large one for the center and two smaller ones that are matching in size.

2 Holding one end of the crossed wires tightly, wrap the wire as closely as possible around the other piece. Make a three-ring coil. Hold the coil in the jaw using flat-nose pliers and twist in the same direction as you coiled. This will tighten the coil to the inner wire.

3 Use the round end of the hammer and a steel block to create a texture at the top of the heart on either side of the center loop. This will strengthen the heart, but take care or the wire will snap. Hammer the center loop gently to flatten it slightly. Cut off any excess wire from beneath the coil at the point of the heart.

4 Working from the roll, take the colored 24-gauge wire and coil it around the larger heart shape at the point. Coil around one side twice, bring the colored wire from the back across to the other copper wire, and wrap from the front around this wire three times. Continue this wrap, adding more coils as the shape widens. Wrap as much of the heart as you wish, then finish with a three-ring coil and snip off the end.

5 Connect the central large heart to the outside ones with the 24-gauge wire, still working from the coil if you find it comfortable. Work out where you want the outside hearts to sit against the central one. At this point, coil the wire three times around the large heart, bring the wire from the back across to the other heart, and wrap from the inside of the smaller heart, around just the smaller one twice, then again from the back across to the larger heart, and wrap twice around this heart. You should end up with three sets of two coils on the large heart and two on the smaller one.

6 Hammer the two 10mm jumprings a little to match and attach to the outsides of the smaller hearts as in Step 5. Attach a complementary chain of the desired length to the jumprings. Finish with a lobster clasp on one side, using the chain on the opposite side as its closer ring, or attach a jumpring. For a dark finish, patina with liver of sulfur if desired (see page 21).

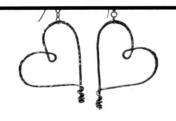

Earrings

YOU WILL NEED

2 x 6in (150mm) lengths of US 16-gauge (SWG 18, 1.25mm) wire, copper

4 x 5mm jumprings, copper

2 x earwires, copper

Make two smaller hearts and hang them from earwires for a matching pair of earrings.

Pendant

YOU WILL NEED

1 x 12in (305mm) length of US 16-gauge (SWG 18, 1.25mm) wire, copper

1 x 39⅜in (1m) length of US 24-gauge (SWG 25, 0.5mm) wire, pink

1 x ready-made fine chain, copper

One heart works well as a pendant. Hang on a finer long chain, suspending the heart from the central loop.

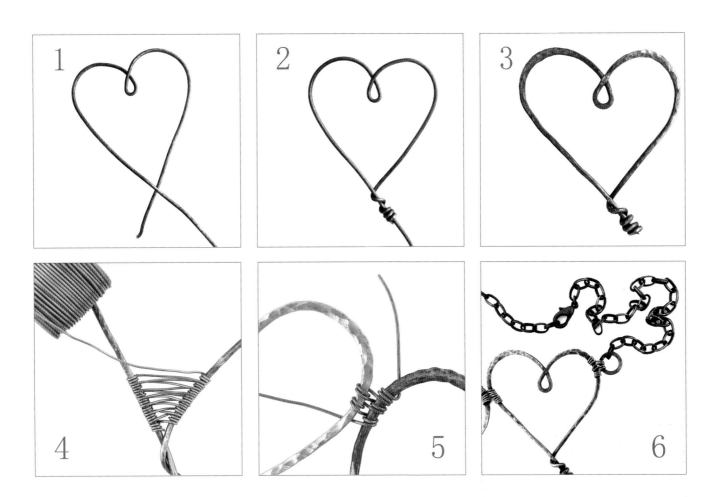

This project is ideal for using up scraps of wire. You could make several small hearts and string them together with cord to make the chain flexible, or vary the shapes—remember, they don't have to be hearts.

Springtime Blooms

Spring will be in the air whatever the weather when you wear this floral set by Sue Mason-Burns. Create a verdant tribute to the classic daffodil in gold wire and delicate spring hues.

FOR THE NECKLACE YOU WILL NEED

1 x reel of US 18-gauge (SWG 19, 1mm) wire, gold-plated

1 x reel of US 28-gauge (SWG 30, 0.3mm) wire, gold-plated

3 x polymer clay daffodil beads

5 x 18mm sieve disks, gold-plated

100 (approx.) x 6mm x 4mm faceted glass beads, green

100 (approx.) assorted 6mm and 4mm beads, greens and golds

6 x crystal drop beads, clear

8 x Lucite flower beads, purple

1 x 4mm x 5mm x 0.8mm crossed chain, gold-plated

13 x 6mm jumprings, gold-plated

3 x 4mm jumprings, gold-plated

1 x trigger clasp, gold-plated

Side cutters

Bent-nose pliers

Round-nose pliers

Chain-nose pliers

Hammer

Steel bench block

Tape

The sieve disks are ideal for covering unsightly wirework at the rear of the design, but they would also make an attractive flower center.

Necklace

1   Flush cut 20in (500mm) of 18-gauge wire. Use a flower template, either drawn or downloaded and printed. Tape one end of the wire to the template along the line of one petal with a ¾in (20mm) overhang. Use your fingers to follow the lines of the template with the wire. Grip the wire with bent-nose pliers to allow you to follow the bends of the petals.

2   Remove the tape and join the wires by laying them parallel and coiling seven times with one end of a 39⅜in (1m) length of 28-gauge wire. Form a loop in the shorter wire tail and a spiral to the longer wire tail. This spiral will form a platform for the daffodil bead to sit on when it is added.

3   Use a hammer on a steel bench block to hammer the wire flower shape flat. This helps the flower to hold its shape because the process of hammering, or forging, both hardens and flattens the wire, giving it rigidity. Do not hammer the coiled section of the flower, as it may break.

4   Thread a daffodil bead onto the 28-gauge wire. With its base sitting on the spiral from Step 2, secure to the opposite side of the flower shape by coiling the wire around the outer wire of the spiral and a curve between two petals. Coil three or four times for security. Using the 28-gauge wire, add faceted green beads, coiling around the frame between each.

5   Add crystal drop beads in the center of each petal by threading the bead, narrow end first, then a 4mm bead. Take the wire outside the 4mm bead, back through the crystal drop bead, and secure to the frame of the flower. Continue adding an assortment of 6mm and 4mm beads, using them to cover any wire that is showing. Secure the beads to the flower frame between additions.

6   Center a sieve disk over the rear of the design, covering where the beads have been secured to the frame. Attach by taking the wire through the outermost holes of the sieve and securing around the flower frame. When all the holes have been sewn through, secure the wire to the frame, and trim. Make two further flowers, slightly smaller in size, omitting the crystal drops.

7   Centre a 4mm bead on the 28-gauge wire and thread both ends through a purple Lucite bead. Take the larger flower and a smaller one, and lay the sieve disk over the ends of a petal of each. Continue adding Lucite flowers with 4mm bead centers to the sieve disk, securing the petal frames as you go. Add 4mm green beads to the sieve disk to cover any gaps.

8   Add a sieve disk to the back of the disk added at Step 7, lining up the holes. Use the wire tail to attach the two disks together through the outermost holes. Add 4mm green beads to each pass of the wire through the holes to cover the edge of the sieve disks, making sure the beads lie at the front of the design. Repeat for the other small flower.

9   Attach three sets of two 6mm jumprings to an upper petal of each smaller flower, attaching each set of two to the previous set. Cut two 5in (120mm) lengths of chain and attach to the last set of jumprings with a 4mm jumpring. Attach the clasp to one end of chain with a 4mm jumpring. Add a 6mm jumpring to the other end of the chain.

Try using the ball end of your hammer to apply texture to your wire design.

Brooch

YOU WILL NEED

1 x 20in (500mm) length of US 18-gauge (SWG 19, 1mm) wire, gold-colored

1 x 39⅜in (1m) length of US 28-gauge (SWG 30, 0.3mm) wire, gold-colored

1 x polymer clay daffodil bead

6 x 8mm crystal drop beads, clear

6 x 4mm crystal bicones, green

30 x 6mm faceted round beads, green and gold-colored

1 x brooch bar, gold-colored

Follow the instructions for the necklace to make the larger central flower and add a brooch back finding, instead of a sieve disk, to the rear of the flower.

Floral Fancy

You can wear flowers on your fingers, wrists or even in your hair with this pretty floral collection by Rachel Murgatroyd. The motif is so versatile it can be used in almost any item of jewelry.

FOR THE RING
YOU WILL NEED

1 x 15¾in (400mm) length of US 18-gauge (SWG 19, 1mm) round wire

1 x 6in (150mm) length of US 26-gauge (SWG 27, 0.4mm) round wire

1 x 8mm focal bead

7 x 5mm accent beads

Ring mandrel

Flat-nose pliers

Side cutters

Ring

1 Wrap five times around the tip of the ring mandrel, starting at approx. 2in (50mm) off the center of your wire. The ends should form a straight line under the five circles, so if you place the mandrel on a table the end wires should be flat with circles above. The position you choose to wrap around will determine the size of your petals and the amount of wire needed.

2 Slide the coils off the mandrel. Using the finer wire bind around the wires. Anchor the finer wire to one of the end wires by wrapping around three or four times. Cut short and smooth down with pliers. Leave the other end long as you will use this later to attach the beads.

3 Place the wires on the ring mandrel as though the circles are a bead at the top of the ring. Wrap the ends around the mandrel and take them back up to the top so they go past the circles. Do not cross the wires; if they start at the top, they should still be at the top after wrapping around the mandrel. The top wire should bend down around the circles and the bottom wire should bend up.

4 Wrap these wires around the bottom of the circles until the ends are at a right angle to the shank of the ring. Carefully slide off the mandrel, keeping the wires as still as possible so the ring is not distorted.

5 Using pliers, wrap the end of the wire through the middle of the ring around the shank once or twice and trim off on the outside or top of the ring and press down. Do this on both sides of the ring. Trim the top outside of the ring so any sharp ends do not press against your finger.

6 Create the flower by separating the circles and using a pair of pliers to bring them down.

7 Once all five of your circles are flat, tweak them with your fingers to get them just right. You could open the two wires on the shank all the way so they are completely flat under the flower and, from the top, look just like two extra petals.

8 Bring the fine wire to the top of the ring through a suitable gap so it is central and add the focal bead. Pass the wire back down into the center of the ring, securing the bead in place. Bring the wire through to the top again and wrap around the bead once or twice until it feels secure.

9 Thread on the accent beads until they surround the central bead. Pass the wire under the accent beads and wrap around the focal bead twice, then pass down through the ring band. Wrap the fine wire around a thicker wire three or four times, then trim and press down.

Hatpin

YOU WILL NEED

1 x 22in (560mm) length of US 18-gauge (SWG 19, 1mm) wire, copper

1 x 6in (150mm) length of US 26-gauge (SWG, 27, 0.4mm) wire, copper

2 x 8mm faceted bead, green

7 x 5mm round beads, amber

Create a hatpin by using 5⅛–6in (130–150mm) of 18-gauge wire, put a loop on one end, add a bead and swirl the wire around in a freeform. Hammer to work-harden and file the end smooth. Make the flower ring following the main steps and flatten the two ring bands out in opposite directions. Use the pin to secure the flower to your hat.

Bracelet

YOU WILL NEED

1 x 16in (400mm) length of US 18-gauge (SWG 19, 1mm) wire, copper

1 x 6in (150mm) length US 26-gauge (SWG 21, 0.4mm) wire, copper

1 x 8mm faceted bead, green

7 x 5mm round beads, amber

1 x 39in (1m) silk ribbon, green and gold

Flatten the ring band loop out in opposite directions. Pass a silk ribbon through the two loops that used to be the ring shank. Bind the ribbon around your wrist.

The focal beads you use can be any size. Try a really big central bead surrounded by smaller beads, or a central square bead with round surrounding it.

Resources

UK

Beads Unlimited
Stockwell Lodge Studios
Rear of 121-131
Conway Street
Hove
East Sussex
BN3 3LW
Tel: +44 (0)1273 740777
www.beadsunlimited.co.uk

Beads Direct Ltd
10 Duke Street
Loughborough
Leicestershire
LE11 1ED
Tel: +44 (0)1509 218028
www.beadsdirect.co.uk

The Bead Shop
44 Higher Ardwick
Manchester
M12 6DA
Tel: +44 (0)161 274 4040
www.the-beadshop.co.uk

Fred Aldous Ltd
37 Lever Street
Manchester
M1 1LW
Tel: +44 (0)161 236 4224
www.fredaldous.co.uk

Bead and Button Company
The Workshop
58 Lower North Road
Carnforth
Lancashire
LA5 9LJ
Tel: +44 (0)1524 720 880
www.beadandbuttoncompany.
co.uk

Palmer Metals Ltd
401 Broad Lane
Coventry
CV5 7AY
Tel: +44 (0)845 644 9343
www.palmermetals.co.uk

Spoilt Rotten Beads
7 The Green,
Haddenham
Ely
Cambridgeshire
CB6 3TA
Tel: +44 (0)1353 749853
www.spoiltrottenbeads.co.uk

Jillybeads
1 Anstable Road
Morecambe
LA4 6TG
Tel: +44 (0)1524 412728
www.jillybeads.co.uk

The Bead Merchant
22 Observer way
Kelvedon
Essex
CO5 9NZ
Tel: +44 (0)1376 570022
www.beadmerchant.co.uk

Bead Aura
3 Neal's Yard
Covent Garden
London
WC2H 9DP
Tel: +44 (0)20 7836 3002
www.beadaura.co.uk

**The Genuine Gemstone
Company Limited**
Unit 2D Eagle Road
Moons Moat
Redditch
Worcestershire
B98 9HF
Tel: +44 (0)800 6444 655
www.jewellerymaker.com

Creative BeadCraft
Unit 2 Asheridge Business
Centre
Asheridge Road
Chesham
Buckinghamshire
HP5 2PT
Tel: +44 (0)1494 778818
www.creativebeadcraft.co.uk

Beadtime
Beadtime Warehouse
Unit 16, Shepperton Business
Park
Govett Avenue
Shepperton
TW17 8BA
Tel: +44 (0)1932 244700
www.beadtime.co.uk

Bijoux Beads
Elton House
2 Abbey Street
Bath
BA1 1NN
Tel: +44 (0)1225 482024
www.bijouxbeads.co.uk

GJ Beads
Unit L
St Erth Industrial Estate
Hayle
Cornwall
TR27 6LP
Tel: +44 (0)1736 751070
www.gjbeads.co.uk

Beadsisters
Mid Cairngarroch Croft
Stoneykirk
Stranraer
Wigtownshire
DG9 9EH
Tel: +44 (0)1776 830352
www.beadsisters.co.uk

Shiney Rocks
14 Sandy Park Road,
Brislington
Bristol
BS4 3PE
Tel: +44 (0)117 300 9800
www.shineyrocks.co.uk

Wires.co.uk
Unit 3 Zone A
Chelmsford Road Industrial
Estate
Great Dunmow
Essex
CM6 1HD
Tel: +44 (0)1371 238013
www.wires.co.uk

USA

Beadin' Path
Tel: +1 207-650-1557
www.beadinpath.com

**Fire Mountain Gems
and Beads**
1 Fire Mountain Way
Grants Pass
OR 97526-2373
Tel: +1 800-355-2137
(toll free)
Tel: +1 541-956-7890
www.firemountaingems.com

**Vintaj Natural Brass
Company**
PO box 246
Galena, Il 61036
www.vintaj.com

Index

To place an order, or to request a catalogue, contact:

GMC Publications Ltd

Castle Place, 166 High Street, Lewes, East Sussex, BN7 1XU

United Kingdom

Tel: +44 (0)1273 488005

Website: www.gmcbooks.com